Silver Witchcraft Tarot

by Barbara Moore
Artwork by Franco Rivolli
Graphic layout by Lo Scarabeo

© Lo Scarabeo 2014

Lo Scarabeo
Via Cigna 110, 1055 - Torino, Italy
E-mail: info@loscarabeo.com
Internet: http://www.loscarabeo.com

Printed by CT printing

First Edition: April 2014

SILVER
WITCHCRAFT
TAROT

BY
BARBARA MOORE

TABLE OF CONTENTS

INTRODUCTION
WELCOME TO THE
SILVER WITCHCRAFT TAROT

The spiritual world and magick are not separate from us. The spirit of the Divine is within everything that exists, seen and unseen, and connects us to each other and everything. We are spiritual beings on this earth having a human experience. There are many definitions for magick, but probably at it's most essential, it's most basic level, magick is being aware of the ebbs and flows of the Universe, the spirits that inhabit it and the energies that swim through it. It is being aware of all of that and being able to work with it, co-creating this experience we call reality.

Being a skilled magick worker is like being skilled at anything, say being a gymnast. You begin training with basic theories that build your understanding of your body and how to move it, as well as how it interacts with the world around you, such as the floor or a balance beam. You learn, in a very real way, about physics and probably develop a deep understanding of and intense love/hate relationship with the law of gravity. Through practice you get better, gain control of yourself and a deeper understanding of how things work. Eventually, you move past basic training and move toward finding your own unique expression within the world of gymnastics; you develop your art. You create reality.

As you develop your art, you learn about yourself and about what kind of visual experience you wish to create. You have your favorite moves, the ones that challenge you, and ones that just make you happy and perhaps some that make you feel particularly strong or fierce. You blend moves with music to create an experience for your audience (or perhaps just for your own enjoyment). You learn what combinations evoke specific responses. Once you can do that, you are closer to becoming a master of your chosen path.

Yet, you never really "arrive" because you continue to change, physically, mentally, emotionally, and spiritually, and so your work, your goals change. It is a journey that continues until it ends. But even if you quit performing, what you've done and learned stays with you and informs who you become in the future and how you move through the world. Anything we choose to do works like this, including our journey of spiritual seeking and magickal work.

Tarot isn't essential to spiritual development or to magickal work. However, for those interested in tarot, it can be a wonderful tool for deepening spiritual and magickal understanding. It is said that witches are walkers between worlds. Tarot is, in so many ways, also a thing that walks between worlds, forming bridges and connections. For example, because it utilizes both symbols and symbolic systems (such as suits, correspondences, and numbers) as well as images, it connects the right brain/intuitive understanding with the left brain/intellectual understanding. When both ways of understanding are engaged, we are at our optimal level for accessing Divine wisdom, whether we are seeking guidance or even predictions.

The Silver Witchcraft Tarot creates a bridge between the world of traditional Rider-Waite-Smith tarot images and meanings and the world of magickal spiritual understanding. Therefore it can be used both for traditional, predictive readings and for meditation, reflection, and study. The lessons it contains, however, are not laid out in any kind of order. There is no syllabus or quizzes. Tarot is a book of seventy-eight loose pages, pages that are meant to be shuffled. These cards are merely doorways to worlds of Divine wisdom. More precisely, they are keys that you use to open the doorways within yourself to find your own Divine wisdom. We are all unique and the lessons we are learning right now are ours alone. So when you shuffle the cards, you allowing the Divine to bring to you the keys you can use to access the knowledge you need right now. The next time you shuffle, your need will be different and therefore your cards will (probably!) be different. Or, as they say, you can never step into the same river twice, so even if you drew the same card, you would not walk through the same door twice. Walking through the first time changes you, so when you face the same door again, it will be a different experience.

So that you can get the most out of your Silver Witchcraft Tarot deck, the book provides for each card traditional upright and reversed keywords, a short musing on the lessons to guide your further musings, and a reflection to take you even deeper. You will also find basic information about the structure of a tarot deck along with the unique variations for this deck, guidance on how to perform a divination, tips on how to use the cards in magickal work, and spreads.

CHAPTER 1:
TAROT BASICS

STRUCTURE

Effective tarot reading is a balance between the intellect and intuition. One of the reasons tarot is such an effective tool is because it engages both sides of the brain. When both sides are working at their best, we are better poised to receive and understand the wisdom presented in the cards. If we neglect one in favor of the other, the neglected side becomes a shadow. When shadows are ignored or repressed, they tend to pop out at inopportune times and get in the way of the work we are trying to do. For example, if we neglect our intellect and focus only on intuitive responses, our rational thought acts like the proverbial "monkey mind" and causes us to question or over think our intuitive reactions. On the other hand, if we focus on only symbolic interpretation, our readings can be dry and lacking in that special something, which is the spark of Divine inspiration.

Structure provides a framework that lets the intellect feel safe and useful. It also helps bring coherence to a reading, helping us to make sense of the intuitive information we receive. An important part of doing an effective tarot reading is communication. Structure helps us to create a story and tie all the pieces together in a way that makes sense. The structure of tarot helps us in several ways. First, the divisions of the deck, make it easier to learn the cards. By matching the suit meaning with the numbers, we can get a quick shorthand for each card. Second, the symbolic elements of the cards, when looked at as an overview before interpreting individual cards, creates an informational framework for the situation.

A tarot deck divides easily into sections. The first division is between the Major and Minor Arcana. The Major Arcana are the twenty-two cards that are marked with a Roman Numeral and a name, such as II, The High Priestess or VI, The Lovers. The names along with the images help give an immediate understanding of the meanings. The High Priestess, with her closed book and secretive look, lets you know right away that she represents wisdom that is felt or experienced rather than read about or understood intellectually. The Lovers lets you know that one of the meanings has to do with union. The Major Arcana cards represent large themes in our lives, milestones, turning points, lessons, or events that are outside of our immediate control or influence and are associated with the element of Spirit.

The Minor Arcana cards represent everyday situations and things that we can more easily control or influence. The Minor Arcana cards are further divided into four suits. Each suit contains an Ace through 10. Each contains as well as four face cards (Page, Knight, Queen, and King) that are called the Court Cards. The Court Cards represent the people in our lives or aspects of ourselves. The suits each govern an area of life. In addition, each suit is usually associated with an element. Here are the suits of the Silver Witchcraft Tarot along with their traditional correspondences and areas of life.

- **Silver Moons** are also known as Cups or Chalices and are associated with Water. They govern emotions and relationships.
- **Silver Threads** are also known as Pentacles and are associated with Earth. They govern the material world.
- **Silver Wings** are also known as Swords and are associated with Air. They govern our thoughts.
- **Silver Flames** are also known as Wands and are associated with Fire. They govern our passions.

In the Silver Witchcraft Tarot, the numbers take on even more meaning than in traditional tarot. They show the cycle of the year through the traditional pagan holidays and the progression of numbers. These associations can be used as timing clues but more importantly are metaphors that can be extrapolated to any situation regardless of time of year. Here are the number associations for the Silver Witchcraft Tarot along with some traditional meanings for the numbers in parentheses.

- **1 is the Self**, the beginning, the seed, the source *(new beginnings or fresh opportunities)*
- **2 is Yule**, the Winter Solstice, a safe world *(choices or relationships)*
- **3 is Imbolc**, the world awakens *(creativity or teamwork)*
- **4 is Ostara**, the Spring Equinox, a moment full of energy *(stability or stagnation)*
- **5 is Beltane**, a world of growing and connecting *(conflict, loss, or chaos)*
- **6 is Litha**, the Summer Solstice, an explosion of beauty *(communication, community, or problem solving)*

- ❧ **7 is Lammas**, the harvest in the world *(reflection or assessment)*
- ❧ **8 is Mabon**, the Autumn Equinox, a world preparing to go to sleep *(movement, speed, or power)*
- ❧ **9 is Samhain**, a world asleep and open spiritual doors *(independence or solitude)*
- ❧ **10 is the Universe**, the greater world *(endings or completion)*

The numbers provide a connection between the suits but also helps highlight their differences. For example, Silver Wings or Air reacts differently to the energy of Mabon than Silver Threads or Earth.

Understanding the Cycle

Too many times, due to cultural influences of the western world, we think linearly: cause to effect, beginning to end, before to after. Nature, and as a consequence the Universe, does not always works like that, but rather creates pattern that are circular in nature: cause to effect to cause, beginning to end to a new beginning, and so on... One immediate consequence of this is that the Universe is less dramatic then we are sometimes (maybe just because the Universe is much older and wiser than mankind)... so it tries to teach us not to linger at the end of any road. Be it success or defeat, the road goes on, and energies will raise and wane naturally.

In the Tarot, the traditional numbering that was developed at the beginning of twentieth century suggests a road from the beginning (the Ace) to the end (the 10), a road that expresses the natural growth of a situation or of a person through trials and challenges until something complete.

Along with the traditional meaning, the Silver Witchcraft Tarot suggests a different road, one that is given to us by the flowing of the seasons.

The 1 and the 10 are not anymore the beginning and the end, but rather they are the self and the greater world surrounding the self. Living, growing, doing, experiencing, is – if you think about it – a continuous exchange of energies between the self and the world. As we do we change the world around us, but the world, in turn, offers experiences that change us. In the 2, the exchange of energies is at the minimum, and it represent a time to gather energies, protect them, wait and rest. The 3, the exchange of energies begins to expand and take strength, until it reaches its peak with the 6. Then begins the time to harvest, to sort things and to slow down, preparing for a new cycle.

The cards of the Silver Witchcraft Tarot takes into account both the tra-
ditional meaning and the cyclic meaning even when they seem occasion-
ally very different. When reading the cards, try to perceive a pattern... to
understand whether in the current moment you need more to focus on a
linear direction (the need for achievement) or to focus on a cyclic direction
(the need for continuity).

In addition to seeing the connections and patterns of the numbers amongst the suits, we can divine further connections and patterns by using the numbers of the Major Arcana cards. For example, II, The High Priestess connects to the 2s. Numbers above ten can be reduced down and further connected. For example, XIII, Death reduces to four (XIII is 13 and $1 + 3 = 4$).

✸ INTUITION ✸

The other half of tarot comes in form of intuitive responses. Tarot cards have pictures on them for a reason. If we were just meant to use the names and numbers, we could just have plain cards with that information printed on them. Even the symbols are not just depicted as simple images like road signs. Instead, we put miniature pieces of art on the cards. We do this because art evokes a different type of response, more personal and emotional.

It is said that dreams are a way for our subconscious to communicate with our conscious mind. Dreams are usually a collection or series of images that may not make sense at first glance, but upon reflection, we find the message we are meant to get. The art on the tarot cards is designed to work in this same way. By marrying these seemingly unrelated images with the order and struc-ture of the deck, we can more easily access the important messages given to us by the Divine through tarot.

Before looking at the meaning of a card on the book, you may choose to
use your intuition and ask yourself "what is happening here?" Finding
your own meaning to a card does not mean "to go random," but it means
to "tune yourself to the energy of the cards." Intuition is a powerful tool...
and it is wise to listen to it. Imagine a card showing a person helping
another... it doesn't matter if all the books in the world suggest that the
meaning of that card is "helping," if your intuition is telling you — every
time you see that card — that the meaning is "receiving help."

This is why it is important to look at the images, and let them tell you a story, suggests images, concepts, situations and emotions. Then, once you have found a connection with the image, try to think over the meaning suggested into the book.

In the end, the rational (what you find in the book) and the intuitive (what is your subjective perception) are not enemies, but dear friends helping each other.

Also, if you read cards to other, remember to accept the intuition of the person you are reading to, especially if it's different from yours. Because a reading will be much better if not just you are talking to the querent, but if the cards are talking as well.

Some people are more comfortable with recognizing their intuitive responses. Others worry about "getting it wrong." Try this: ask a simple question, like "what do I need to know right now about working with the Silver Witchcraft Tarot," shuffle the cards, and draw one. Try not to attend to the name or number and instead just focus on the image. Note your immediate response to the art. Try to articulate your answer based on the image along. Now try it with three cards, merging the cards together into one cohesive answer. If you find yourself coming up with answers very easily, you are probably more comfortable with trusting your intuitive reactions. If you struggled and worried you were doing it wrong, you can become more comfortable with practice.

This is a skill you'll want to develop because not only will it help you give better readings but it will also help you meditate with the cards. You can use the cards as doorways to explore deeper spiritual meanings. The cards will become starting points for you to develop your own unique understanding of both your spiritual practice and your interpretations for the cards that go far beyond anything found in this or any book.

REVERSALS

Reversals are cards that appear upside down in a reading. Some readers incorporate reversals by shuffling their decks in a way to ensure that some cards appear reversed. Other readings shuffle carefully to make sure all the cards are upright. This is a matter of personal choice. Reversed meanings are provided and can be used if you wish. Some readers who use reversals do not use traditional reversed meanings but instead use a system that applies to reversed cards. Such systems include reading the reversed cards as blocked, repressed, stagnate, or internalized energy.

If you decide not use reversals but one shows up in a reading, you can decide to pay special attention to that card, as if it were behaving like a trickster and demanding special emphasis. Alternately, you can simply turn it upright and read it as usual.

CHAPTER 2:
HOW TO DO A READING

≫ DIVINATION ≪

Most people acquire a tarot deck because they want to perform divinations. They idea of knowing the future is a heady one. How much easier, how much more gloriously successful, would our lives be if we could only know the future! Indeed, things may be easier. The truth of the matter is that the future is not set in stone, which is a coupe for free will and self-determination but it is not so helpful when trying to divine the future. This does not mean tarot readings are useless. On the contrary, they can be very helpful as long as you understand what is possible and what isn't possible. Think about weather forecasts. The weather report for tomorrow is usually pretty reliable, as long as there aren't too many chaotic things going on in the atmosphere. The more moving parts, as it were, the less reliable. The further out you look, the less reliable the forecast because in the intervening days, things can change thereby creating a different future.

As you look at your own life questions, keep in mind that the further out you look, the less certain your answers. The more complicated a situation, that is, the more that is going on and the more people involved, the more volatile and therefore more changeable a situation. While the cards may not be able to tell you exactly what is going to happen, they can help you understand how you think and feel about a situation and they can help you make decisions based on those thoughts and feelings, taking into account the energy surrounding the situation.

Before delving into a reading, think about what you want to know. And think about why you want to know. A cardinal rule of tarot is "don't ask if you don't want to know." As you are forming your question, consider for a moment what you would consider possible answers, including the ones that would disappoint you the most. If that were the answer, how would you respond? Would the information truly be helpful to you? Think about what kind of information would be the most useful and how you would use it in your life. Use that to guide your question asking.

After you've settled on your question, think about what spread you want to use. The spread should be one that will provide the information you need. Some of the spreads in this book are designed to be used for a wide range of questions and can be easily adapted for specific situations. Do not be afraid to alter or even invent a spread to suit your purposes. Some spreads do not require a question as they are designed for specific uses.

Reflection

To be a good reader, a person need to treat Tarot with respect. But respect is not reverence. Tarot can be serious, and Tarot can be light. In order to gain mastery with the cards, it's often useful to use the cards for very light questions, which carry only a small fraction of an emotional burden. It's kind of obvious that a question "What kind of impression do I want to give?" while choosing a dress for tonight is lighter when going out for a pizza with friends, rather then when going to a first date with someone you truly love. Small things are essential to pave the road to bigger things. Do not jump though, but rather build your tarot experience with many small questions, possibly one each day, in order to be able to get true assistance from the Tarot when you need it badly.

The "card of the day" method, is truly useful for this. Just draw a card in the morning asking yourself "what should I pay attention to today?" and then think it over in the evening. It takes 5 minutes, it's fun, it's useful, and if done honestly it builds a huge amount of Tarot experience in very little time. Also, "attention" is one of the keys to the soul, because only when we pay attention – when we are really present to something or to someone -, the soul can touch and be touched by the world.

Because we consider readings as dialogues with the Divine, we usually treat the experience with some reverence by incorporating rituals. The amount and type of ritual depends on you. For some, a simple clearing off of table space, a few cleansing breaths, a moment of centering, and short prayer or statement of intent are all that is needed. For some, a more elaborate set up is preferred, for example setting up a small divination altar and casting a circle. Maybe some readings will require simple rituals while others, say a yearly birthday or holiday spread or one about potential magickal work, will be best served by something more formal. You know yourself and your relationship with the Divine. Do what best suits your practice and beliefs.

When you are ready, shuffle your cards and lay them out on the table as indicated by the spread. You can deal off the top or fan them out and select the cards that way. While you can lay the cards face down, it is more useful to lay them all face up so you can develop a general overview and create a framework for the reading.

To create a framework for the answer, look at all the cards together and analyze the types of cards and their numbers. By doing so, you can learn a lot about the situation and begin to bring order to the information provided. Each element of the deck means something. The list below is a good guide. It doesn't take long to do this and the benefits are worth the effort. A tarot deck has balance of proportion built into it. If any of the elements seems out of proportion or inappropriate to the situation, you should investigate this further and take it into account in your final reading.

A reading, as we mentioned, provides a forecast. One of the things we seek is an understanding of the energies present. We also want to know to what extent we can influence or effect a situation. One of the most important things we learn from analyzing the reading as a whole is ease with which we can change the course of events. Understanding the type of energy present can help us make better decisions and use our own energy more effectively.

❧ A. Look for reversals
If you use reversals, you are probably familiar with the percentage of reversed cards that normally come up in a reading. If there is a disproportionate number, it can indicate that the situation is blocked or that there are challenges that prohibit the flow of events.

❧ B. Look for Major Arcana cards
These cards represent energy and events beyond the your control. If there are a disproportionate number in the reading (more than one third), you have less control over events and are likely in the midst of learning an important life lesson.

❧ C. Look for the Court cards
If there are a disproportionate number of court cards (more than about twenty percent), too many people are involved in the situation or you are having issues as to how to behave or react. If the reading (and situation) feels confused, start weeding out the influences of others and bring the focus back on yourself.

∾ D. Analyze the suits present

Are the four suits equally represented? If not, what does that say about the situation? If many Silver Wings are present, you may be too much in your head. Lots of Silver Moons, then perhaps the situation is fraught with emotions. The lack of Silver Moons in a relationship reading can mean a lack of true feelings and intimacy. When developing advice about the situation, seek ways to bring balance, if necessary.

In terms of analyzing the mutability of a situation, Air and Fire are considered active elements and are characterized by being fast moving. So Wings and Flames would indicate a more active and potentially chaotic situation. Water and Earth are considered passive elements and are characterized by being slow moving. Moons and Threads, therefore, would indicate a stable situation and potentially stagnant energy that could be harder to turn around.

The Major Arcana cards all have elemental associations as well and so you can use those when assessing the energy represented by the suits.

∾ E. Check the numbers

If there is more than one of any particular number in the spread, pay attention to those associations. For example:

◈ If there are multiple Aces, there is a focus on new beginnings or fresh opportunities.
◈ If there are multiple Twos, there is a focus on choices or relationships.
◈ If there are multiple Threes, there is a focus on creativity or teamwork.
◈ If there are multiple Fours, there is a focus on stability or stagnation.
◈ If there are multiple Fives, there is a focus on conflict, loss, or chaos.
◈ If there are multiple Sixes, there is a focus on communication, community, or problem solving.
◈ If there are multiple Sevens, there is a focus on reflection or assessment.
◈ If there are multiple Eights, there is a focus on movement, speed, or power.
◈ If there are multiple Nines, there is a focus on independence or solitude.
◈ If there are multiple Tens, there is a focus on something coming to an end.

You can use the numbers in a different way as well. Oftentimes in a reading, we want to see what a situation is like and to see how we might change the outcome. Knowing how far advanced a situation is lets us know how easily we might change the outcome. For example, if a relationship is in the early stages, consisting of just a few casual dates, it is very simple to end that relationship. The longer a relationship goes on, the more the lives of the couple become intertwined and the more energy it takes to end that relationship.

- If there are a large number of aces, twos, and/or threes, the situation is in early stages of development and most easily influenced or changed.
- If there are a large number of fours, fives, and/or sixes, the situation in the middle phase and will require more effort to change.
- If there are a large number of sevens, eights, and/or nines, the situation is well entrenched and will require considerable effort to change.
- If there are a large number of tens, the situation nearly resolved and may be very difficult (although not necessarily impossible) to change.

F. Look at the visual pattern made by the cards

Step back and look at your reading as one large picture. Look at the colors. What do they tell you about the situation? Look for repeated symbols and consider their significance.

G. Interpret individual cards

Once you've scanned the reading as a whole, interpret the individual cards keeping in mind the question asked and the positional meaning as defined by the spread you selected as well as the information already gathered.

> Reflection
>
> *You may have noticed that there is a constant element reappearing in the Silver Witchcraft Tarot: the duality between complementary opposites or points of view. For instance between "pattern" and "detail", or between "book meaning" and "intuitive meaning" or between "self "and "the greater world".*
>
> *When you read the cards into a spread, you will have the individual cards on one side, each with its own meaning and suggestions. And you will have a bigger picture, of the spread as a whole, where you can see patterns and connections.*
>
> *It would be nice if we could give an answer like a recipe on how to merge the gestalt meaning (a meaning that comes from pattern and from the cards as a whole) and the detailed meanings (the sum of the individual meaning of the cards). But a recipe or a rule, even if brilliant and devised by the best Tarot reader in the world, would be ultimately wrong. The big and the small, the here and the there, the above and the below, always coexist. They touch each other, they affect each other, but they never trump each other. True balance is the most difficult thing, because it cannot be ruled and quantified.*

Despite, this, do not be scared to try as there is no way to do wrong.

When learning Tarot, if you find yourself looking too much to the individual meaning, make an effort to look more at patterns and at the whole. But if you look too much to the whole spread and see many patterns, sometimes focus on details and look at one thing at a time. And balance will came to you.

Balance – not just in Tarot – is not chosen, but found.

✦ FURTHER TIPS FOR CLEAR READINGS ✦

◦ Avoid clarifiers

A clarifier is a card that many readers pull in addition to the cards dealt in the reading. These "extra cards" are meant to clarify a card that a reader finds problematic in the reading. Clarifiers are overused and often add to the perceived confusion rather than actually adding understanding. They can become a crutch to avoid a card that is not particularly liked or understood. Instead, try to stick with the cards that are present. They are there for a reason. If you are well and truly stuck, let the reading sit for a day or two and come back to it with fresh eyes. Or meditate on the card that is causing the roadblock. Memorize the card, close your eyes, and step into the card. Ask any characters or creatures present the questions you have about the card. The ego has ways of protecting itself, so the card may contain wisdom that the ego is not willing to hear. Going into a meditative state may make it easier to quell the ego and find the treasure in what at first glance appears to be an unfathomable or troubling card.

◦ End strong

No matter what the outcome of the reading, include an action step. While there are some things truly beyond your control, no matter what happens, you always have the opportunity to take some kind of action or learn some kind of lesson. End the reading with optimism and sense of empowerment.

◦ Eliminate spinning a reading

Sometimes we know what answer we want from the cards. Because the cards have many possible meanings, we can take this too far and convince ourselves of a specific message. One way to avoid this is to think about your desired answer ahead of time. Imagine what cards would best turn up to create that answer. Imagine what cards might represent other answers. After you lay out the cards, look for the ones that you noted for each answer. Read the cards that are there and consider why those specific cards turned up.

CHAPTER 3:
OTHER USES FOR TAROT

Tarot cards are the perfect tool for divination, but they are not just a one trick pony. The cards can be used for other purposes as well.

∼ MAGICKAL WORK ∼

It is beyond the scope of this book to teach magickal practice. If you are uncertain, there are plenty of excellent books on the subject and online resources. As always, make sure you are getting your information from a reliable source.

The cards can be used in magickal workings. For example, you can use the cards to create a portable altar. The four aces can be used to represent the elements/directions. The Empress and the Emperor can be used to represent the Goddess and God. You can select other cards as appropriate and as needed to represent other items.

The cards can be used as focal points for spells. Select one to three cards to represent what you wish to accomplish and leave them on your altar until your spell is completed.

You can charge the cards as talismans and carry one with you for as long as you need.

∼ JOURNALING ∼

Any tarot deck is great as a journaling companion. Draw any card and it can provide you with countless ideas and prompts for self-reflection and spiritual exploration. The Silver Witchcraft Tarot can also provide more focused reflection and study.

As you prepare for an upcoming Sabbat, you can use the card from each suit relating to that holiday as a starting point. For example, if you are preparing for Imbolc, you can take the 3s from each suit and compare and contrast them, using the lessons and reflections as starting points. You can even bring in the corresponding Major Arcana card(s) as well, in this case the Empress, the Hanged Man, and the Universe.

You will notice in next chapter that the Major Arcana cards have two sets of associations. The first is Spheres of Existence: the Material Sphere, the Immaterial/Intellectual Sphere, and the Spiritual/Divine Sphere. Using the cards associated with each of these divisions can provide a springboard for studying each of these realms. The Major Arcana cards are also associated with Areas of Being: the Unknown, Magick, Goddess, God, Universe, Balance, and Energy. Using the cards associated with any of these will create an interesting exploration of those realms.

⚞ MEDITATION ⚟

Meditation or reflection is a powerful way to access your own wisdom and connect with the Divine wisdom. Through meditation, you can receive answers and guidance in a very direct and experiential way. Using the cards as portals will help focus your meditations, giving your experience a clear intent. If you are having trouble with a particular card, if a card keeps coming up in readings, or if you are simply interested or intrigued by a card, meditate with or reflect on it.

Here is an easy and effective technique. Look at your selected image until you have it fixed in your imagination so strongly that you can see it even with your eyes closed. Think about what kind of questions you have about the card or that you would like to ask any of the figures in the card. Find a place where you won't be disturbed. You may wish to meditate in silence, with light music, or with drumming. Assume your preferred meditation posture, usually lying flat or seated with arms and legs uncrossed and feet flat on the ground. Close your eyes. Take three long, slow breaths to calm your heart, mind, and body. Picture the card in your mind, allowing it expand becoming life-size and filling your view. Imagine yourself stepping into the image. Begin to explore. Interact with any characters you find there, asking the questions you prepared ahead of time, if any. When you are done, thank the characters for their help, and write about the experience in your journal or Book of Shadows.

CHAPTER 4:
THE MAJOR ARCANA

The cards of the Major Arcana are the broad brush strokes of our lives. They are the births, deaths, marriages, divorces, new jobs, lost jobs, revelations, vocational callings, and milestones that create the framework for our lives. They are the events by which we reckon time, such as "we did that before we bought this house" or "that happened after the baby was born." These are things that we create and work toward, such as graduation or starting a business. These are also things that happen to us, such as being offered an amazing opportunity or a health crisis. These are, in short, the "big" things, happy, sad, and everything in between.

The characters of the Major Arcana are often called archetypes, reoccurring symbols or motifs from the collective unconscious that live in all our psyches. Like all symbols, they are rich and sometimes filled with contradictions. And like all symbols, they have general interpretations as well as very personal one. They are complex cards and many readers spend their entire tarot career studying the cards without ever finding the edges. They are alive within our souls and alive in the world, and they are ever-changing (even as they are ever-constant) just as our souls and the world is ever-changing.

No one tarot deck and no single book can capture the fullness of these cards. Any tarot deck, any single image can only portray a facet, just as any deity portrays a single facet of the God or Goddess. But any image is just a key for you to use to open the door within yourself to the individual and vast worlds of each archetype. Any words written about them are sign posts pointing you toward possible paths.

That said, there are traditional meanings and conventional interpretations that most students use as a base. They are derived from decades of evolution through the minds and practices of tarot readers and teachers through the years, based on practical experience, spiritual reflection, and philosophical inquiry. This book contains these as well as ideas unique to the Silver Witchcraft Tarot, designed to resonate with magickal practitioners.

For each card, we give the Sphere of Existence, the Area of Being, the astrological association, the elemental association, description, interpretation, a reflection, and keywords for the upright and reversed meanings.

❧ Spheres of Existence
❖ Cards from 1 to 7 relate to the **Material Sphere**
❖ Cards from 8 to 14 relate to the **Immaterial/Intellectual Sphere**
❖ Cards from 15 to 21 relate to the **Spiritual/Divine Sphere**

> Reflection
> *Most of the Major Arcana are shown on a cube. The cube is a battered stone cube in the Material Sphere, as old and worn as earth itself. The cube of the Intellectual Sphere is polished and perfect, as similar to an idea of a cube as it is possible. And finally in the Spiritual Sphere the cube is made of energy.*
>
> *You will also notice that the Material Sphere Arcana are more earthy and solid, while the Spiritual Sphere Arcana are almost abstract figures.*
>
> *When you get these cards in a reading, a very easy way to use the division between Material, Intellectual and Spiritual Spheres – without complicated and somewhat unpractical metaphysical thinking – is to think like this:*
> *Material Sphere Arcana: look around you*
> *Intellectual Sphere Arcana: look inside yourself*
> *Spiritual Sphere Arcana: look at something Greater than you and your surroundings*
>
> *However, metaphysical considerations may be unpractical, but it doesn't mean they are not important. Just choose the right moment for reflecting on them.*

❧ Areas of Being
❖ Arcana I, X and XV are connected to the **Unknown**
❖ Arcana II; XII and XVII are connected with **Magick**
❖ Arcana III, XI and XVIII are connected with the **Goddess**
❖ Arcana IV, VIII and XIX are connected with the **God**
❖ Arcana V, IX and XX are connected with the **Universe**
❖ Arcana VI, XIV, XXI are connected with **Balance**
❖ Arcana VII, XIII, XVI are connected with **Energy**

Reflection
What these things are? It's a very important question.

Even if we call the Arcana "Archetypes", it is not perfectly true. The Mother is an archetype. In the Tarot, however, we do not have a single mother card, but more then one. The Empress is often seen as the Mother, as she expresses and contains the nurturing, life giving energy of the Archetype. But the Empress is actually just one facet of the Archetype. In the Silver Witchcraft, for instance, the Empress represents the Goddess (the Mother is actually one facet of the Goddess) as manifested in the material world. Justice is the same archetypical energy but is manifested in the Intellectual world. And finally that energy is shaped as the Moon when in the Spiritual world.

The Unknown – the Magician, the Wheel and the Devil – represents those energies that we have no label for, and that we cannot understand or accept fully. In the Magician the Unknown is looking at the world, but no matter what her skill and knowledge the Universe will always be greater. In the Wheel the Unknown is expressed by randomness, by things that happen unexpected and that – no matter how hard we look – we can find no reason for them. In the Devil, the Unknown represents the dark side of each spirit... like a dark mirror we are truly afraid to look into.

Magick – the High Priestess, the Hanged Man and the Star – is the language of the Universe (not much different from what many scientists says that Mathematics is). In the High Priestess we access the threshold of learning and understanding magick. In the Hanged Man, we experience that learning and we accept it in our body and mind, as we take magick into ourselves. And in the Star we look toward the Infinite, and we let the Infinite look into us.

The Goddess is the female, receptive, nurturing energy of the Universe. Many times the Goddess is expressed as a Maiden, a Mother and a Crone, as she has three aspects. As the Empress she is representing the nurturing energies of the body. As Justice, she represents the nurturing energies of the mind. And as the Moon, the nurturing energies of the soul.

The God is the male, assertive and creative energy of the Universe. The God has many aspects as well, but usually its energy is a candle burning, then it dies and reborn again. The Emperor is the creative energies of the body, Strength is the creative energy of the mind, and the Sun is the creative energy of the soul.

The Universe is something greater than man. Still it is expressed by the High Priest as the connection between the Divine and man. By the Hermit as the continuous research of man, for the Universe within themselves. And by Judgement as the "one and the whole" connection between the Divine and our soul.

Balance is the coexistence of opposites. It is the understanding that the Universe is not to be divided in good or bad, but that everything just is. The Lovers express Balance as the balance between man and woman, a symbol itself of the conciliation for all of the material complementarities. Temperance is the balance of ideas, of beliefs, of perceptions, of languages, of points of view... and the World is Balance seen as "all in one"... because to the soul, Balance is a state of being, not a choice.

Energy is the connection between everything. It flows constantly and changes shape, like the music sung by the Divine. Where Balance is coexistence, Energy is transformation. In the Chariot Energy is seen as opposites meeting to creating something new. And that something new opens the door to something greater (it is not by mere chance that the Chariot is at the boundary between the Material world and the Intellectual world). Death is another threshold, symbolized by the ultimate passage that leaves nothing unchanged. And Tower is the transformation of the soul, that – at the same time – is destruction and healing.

Of all the cards, one only is still missing: the Fool: the Fool is the journey itself. The Fool is the road, and it is us... walking on it... in happiness or sorrow, wisdom or blindness, awareness or drowsiness.

❧ I . THE MAGICIAN ☙

Material
The Unknown
Astrological: Mercury
Element: Air

Description: *A woman wearing a ritual robe is sitting cross legged on the cube and looking at the starry night. She holds an open Book of Shadows in her hand and points to the stars upward with the other hand. On her right hand she has a bracelet with four pendants: a moon, a coin, a wand, and an athame. The moon is behind her and even though it is night, she glows with such a light that between her and the moon, it doesn't seem dark.*

Traditionally, the Magician card was a Con Man, someone who played tricks on people, usually with selfish intent. More recently, the Magician has been elevated to someone who is well versed in magickal skills, or skills that may seem magickal. But we forget that the Magician is Arcanum I, the beginning, and in many ways one of the first stages in magickal understanding. She reads from a book to learn the concepts of magick. She practices what she learns, becoming accustomed to recognizing the ebb and flow of the Universe and to identifying the individual elements.

The Magician understands that magick is the art and craft of creating change in the world, of co-creating with the Universe. As she practices and experiments, not just reading but interacting with the energies and spirits, she learns that magick is deeper than that. She realizes that the most profound magick takes place within herself. By bringing herself into alignment with her own divine nature, she becomes a channel for the Divine in the world.

She is associated with the number I and with the Unknown because this too is her great secret: No matter how much she learns or what she accomplishes, she will always be surprised by the Universe and by herself. The Divine is a mystery and the Magician's life is an expression of that mystery.

Reflection
Think about the connection between "Above" and "Below". Is the Magician reading the book? Or writing the book? Is she reading the book, or is she reading the Moon and the Stars? One of her hands point to the sky, while the other points to the book. Even if the connection between Above and Below is unseen, it doesn't make it any less real.

Keywords: will, talent, skill, creativity, manifestation, communication, magick, action, awareness, power, resourcefulness, concentration, eloquence

Reversed: trickery, manipulation, deceit, con, liar, misuse of gifts

≈ II . HIGH PRIESTESS ≈

Material
Magick
Element: Water
Astrological: Moon

Description: *The High Priestess sits on a cube between two trees, one covered in white flowers, the other in black. She dips her bare foot into a pool of water reflecting the moon. She holds a closed book and wears symbols for the triple Goddess on her head and chest. Behind her is a veil with a pentagram on it. Although it is night, light spills from behind the veil and emanates from the High Priestess.*

Witchcraft is not a faith-based religion. We do not simply believe things to be true. Instead we know things to be true based on direct experience. We can read, research, and debate all we want, but nothing teaches like experience. The High Priestess guards the threshold of initiation. It is time to close the book, enter the world of mystery, and discover our personal responses to what we find there.

The High Priestess understands the liminal space between opposites, a place where the physical and spiritual realms meet. She understands the flow of water, the cycles of the moon, and the ever-changing nature of the future. Consequently, this card tells us that there is something we are not meant to know at this time. We must travel through the experience without knowing the outcome. This experience tests the knowledge we've accumulated by providing an opportunity to put what we know into practice and thereby turn knowledge into revelation and wisdom.

Reflection
The High Priestess reflects our need for understanding the Universe. Her realm is beyond simply knowing and it's not about the brain and notions. She rules the realm of wisdom and experience. She helps us find meaning in what happens to us, to what we feel, express, receive, observe and do. This experience is not about the ability to learn, but the ability of being able to actually grow based on what we have learnt…in a word, wisdom.

Magick is in the world; it is in the whole universe. It comes into our experience, in the material world, as something wonderful and greater than us. The High Priestess is the channel that links what is Above to what is Below.

Keywords: secrets, initiation, mystery, silence, wisdom, understanding, intuition, insight, subconscious, unrevealed future

Reversed: shallow knowledge, secrets, hidden agendas, passion, conceit

ᴿ III . EMPRESS ᴿ

Material
The Goddess
Astrological: Venus
Element: Earth

Description: *A young maiden in regal but simple robes is standing on a cube with the sun shining upon her. Near her there is a bunny and a few little bunnies. There is an eagle flying in the sky. She has a crown on her head and she holds a long ribbon in her hands. The ribbon flows off the edge of the card on the right and her gaze follows the ribbon.*

The Empress, along with her bunny companions, represents abundance, nature, and growth. And while she honors the wildness of nature, she also brings the aspect of control with her. She is an Empress, a ruler with much responsibility. If some things grow too wild, if they become out of control, then other things don't have enough, and so she keeps an eye on how everything progresses. She, like the eagle, is long-sighted and understands the ebb and flow of life.

Her pink ribbon connects her to the Emperor, with whom she stands, under the same sun, working for the same greater good. Within the cycles of the year, she generates new life, and from her, there will always be more to take the place of that which, of necessity, must die. Life will continue on and while she cares for each individual bunny, she also understands that sometimes there must be a sacrifice for the greater good. Nature never stays still. It is always changing from birth to maturity to death. She changes as needed to nurture all living things through all the cycles of life.

We would do well to remember this in our lives and be grateful for the generous bounty we enjoy while recognizing that if a sacrifice is required, it is for something greater than our own immediate comfort.

Reflection
While the High Priestess expresses female energies under the light of the moon, the Empress is about similar energies but under the light of the sun. Her nurturing energy becomes more friendly, warm and approachable as she seeks the connection with us. She understands her limitations, and she knows she is completed only through the Emperor, but even if that could be true, she doesn't lose her identity and sense of self, because she is as necessary to him as he is to her.

Keywords: abundance, fertility, creativity, pleasure, beauty, happiness, comfort, nature, motherhood, mother, nurturing, love, pregnancy, generosity

Reversed: dependence, co-dependence, laziness, stagnation, smothering, stubbornness, creative block, gluttony

✖ IV . THE EMPEROR ✖

Material
The God
Astrological: Aries
Element: Fire

Description: *A young muscular man in regal but simple robes is standing on a cube with the sun overhead. Near him there is a ram with a few little lambs. He has a crown on his head and holds a long ribbon in his hands. The ribbon crosses over the border of the card on the left. He looks to the left.*

Here the Emperor stands with a ram, the symbol for Aries, the astrological sign with which he is associated. Both the Emperor and Aries embody power and determination. Their strength of character is supported by their resources; their resources are controlled by their character. The true Emperor focuses on his responsibility rather than on his power. For him, power is merely a tool that allows him to fulfill his duty to his people and to the land.

He is pictured with lambs as well as a ram, for he is shepherd, a steward. All that he has is not his but only held and managed for others. His red ribbon connects him to his partner, his other half, the Empress. Together they generate and manage life and resources for the greatest good of the group or society. While she changes with the ebb and flow of life, he tries to maintain stability and balance. Grains, fruits and vegetables only grow in the summer yet people must eat in the winter as well. Maintaining a consistent flow of nourishment in an ever-changing environment is his challenge and his gift. Likewise, we recognize the flow of nature while recognizing our needs as humans. Resources must flow in and out and yet we must make sure we have enough to survive during times of draught.

Together, the Emperor and the Empress, the God and the Goddess, represent the two sides of the great Divine Spirit and through them, we learn of that Spirit and of ourselves and the ties that bind us to each other.

Reflection
The Emperor is a mirror to the Empress. While the High Priest expresses male energies under the light of the moon, the Emperor is about similar energies, but under the light of the sun. His life force energy is strong, straight and warm as he creates, lead and protect. He understands his limitations, and he knows he is completed only through the Empress, but even if that could be true, he doesn't lose his identity and sense of self, because he is as necessary to her as she is to him.

Keywords: Stability, structure, power, authority, leadership, control, protection, stewardship, order, leadership, boss, fatherhood, father, ambition, reason, logic, confidence

Reversed: tyranny, rigidity, inflexibility, controlling, cruelty, abuse of power, poor leadership, undisciplined

V . THE HIGH PRIEST

Material
The Universe
Astrological: Taurus
Element: Earth

Description: *A man is dressed similarly to High Priestess, but wearing a pontiff's hat and a solar pendant. He is sitting in the same spot as the High Priestess and in the same pose, however, the book in his lap is open, there is no water at his feet but rather a sylph, an undine, a salamander, and a gnome stand on the verdant grass before him.*

Just as the Emperor and Empress are paired, the High Priestess and the High Priest also form a complimentary pairing. While she represents wisdom gained through direct experience, he governs the realm of understanding on a conscious level. The wisdom of the High Priestess is felt, within the soul, within the body, in a way that is not always easy to articulate. The gift of the High Priest is that of understanding, for this wisdom must be understood with the mind if it is be lived in this world. It does no good to have all the spiritual experiences possible if we still walk the earth in our old, unenlightened way, treating ourselves, each other, and the world without love and respect.

The High Priest holds the liminal space between the physical and spiritual worlds, just as the High Priestess does. However, his focus is on the material world. He does not guard the entrance to the initiation but rather marks the exit. He provides the teaching and guidance to help us externalize the inner experience of initiation. He helps us change our lives to reflect what we've learned. Through the experience and ideas of those who've gone before us, we learn how to put our spiritual beliefs into practice. We make them real by living them in this world.

The representatives of the elemental energies gather around the High Priest. They both his teachers and his helpers. Like any good teacher, the High Priest is also always a student. As we practice seeing, hearing, and feeling the energies that course through our world, we are being taught by High Priest and his aides.

Reflection
While in the High Priestess card the book is closed, the same book appears open in the High Priest. Enter and exit, Magick and the Universe... they still are connections between the Divine and the Material. The High Priest is about using wisdom in our lives. This is why the book is open. But if this were to be the end of the journey and not the beginning, it would have been the arrogance of mankind, believing that they can label the Divine. But as it is the beginning, it is just the humble mankind, trying to give space to the Divine in their lives as best as they can.

Keywords: education, teaching, learning, knowledge, conformity, tradition, institutions, group identity, values, guidance, orthodoxy, rites, blessing, status quo, social conventions

Reversed: fundamentalism, repression, intolerance, fear, guilt, extremism, restriction, cults, abuse of position

⚜ VI . THE LOVERS ⚘

Material
Balance
Astrological: Gemini
Element: Air

Description: *A man and a woman stand on a cube clasping hands. A ribbon ties their wrist together. She wears a crescent moon pendant and he wears a sun pendant. They are gaze at each other.*

In the Lovers card, this traditional hand-fasting is metaphoric. As a symbol, it is layered with meanings and ramifications. While it may not appear to be so at first glance, within this depiction of a marriage is the seed of the most traditional meanings for Arcana VI, which was, once upon a time, called The Lover and showed a man choosing between two women. The meaning was "choice." The idea of choice is still inherent in this image, although here it seems the choice has already been made. The choices represented by the Lovers involve a balance of deep and sincere consideration as well as passionate longing.

Which brings us to another meaning of the card: the union of opposites. The woman, with her moon necklace, and the man, with his sun pendant, represent the union of opposites, lunar and solar, male and female, joined together by conscious choice, free will, and pure hearts. They come together in perfect harmony and create something greater than the sum of their parts, something new and unique, with a life of its own. Once created, they bear the responsibility of caring for it, nurturing it, protecting it, and above all, honoring it. Tied in with choices is the idea of responsibility for those choices.

The Lovers card reminds you to follow the yearnings of our heart but to also follow up those yearnings with clear thought, being fully conscious of the consequences of your actions, and finally to commit with your whole self, body, mind, heart, and spirit.

Reflection
Opposites are difficult to join. They turn and revolve and dance around one other. But as long as they are balanced, they are connected and they are able to create a greater whole. Even the most simple choice... the choice of love... is not made in one instant, but is to be lived through for a whole cycle. It may be the love for a husband or wife, or for a son or mother... but however we decide to look at it, Love is the language of Balance. It is what makes Balance possible.

Keywords: choices, crossroads, trust, communication, relationships, partnerships, togetherness, love, affection, sexuality, harmony, engagement, attraction, duality

Reversed: separation, disharmony, suspicion, jealousy, obsession, infidelity, fear of commitment, loss of love

∞ VII . THE CHARIOT ∞

Material
Energy
Astrological: Cancer
Element: Water

Description: *A white man and a black woman in ritual robes stand on a cube and holding up their child to the sun. The child is swaddled and his hand pointing upward. In the direction the child is pointing there are stars shining in a daytime sky.*

"Per aspera, ad astra." A rough translation of this is "through hardships to the stars" or "a rough road leads to the stars." The Chariot speaks of this challenge. Finding balance or bringing opposites into union is not always easy. It is, however, essential, in order to move forward. Our spiritual path includes recognizing and synthesizing opposites and it is also a main lesson of tarot. We recognize the male and female, the yin and the yang, within the Great Spirit, within ourselves, and within the world. We learn to value them both. Even in tarot reading, we activate opposing ways of knowing, the intellect and the intuitive, in order to access higher wisdom.

When we are able to do that, when both sides of our nature pull together as a team, moving in the same direction, then we experience breakthroughs in understanding. We see a new path that can lead us forward, like the baby here, pointing the way to the stars, to our higher nature.

The secret is to recognize that opposites hold within themselves the seed of its opposite and that they cannot exist without the other. They are twin reflections that complete each other and give birth to something new.

> Reflection
> *Often the Chariot is seen as triumph or success, as the ultimate expression of the forward momentum that comes from human ambition and greed and need for achievement. A powerful force, and yet, just as often, an illusion. In the Silver Witchcraft, the Chariot is created through love... a love that binds opposites and creates a new energy able to bring you forward. It is not just about overcoming obstacles and winning challenges but about transcending them and opening doors to a bigger world.*

Keywords: drive, ambition, control, direction, determination, success, triumph, victory, will, movement, progress, speed, travel, conquest, battle

Reversed: lack of control, delay, opposition, stagnation, no direction, aggression, cancelled trip, car trouble

❧ VIII . STRENGTH ❧

Intellectual
The God
Astrological: Leo
Element: Fire

Description: *A man holding a Green Man mask is stands on a cube with a lion on his side. He gently lays his hand on the Lion's Mane as if on a pet.*

There are many kinds of strength. The strength of the tarot is not about brute force. Rather, it reflects something even more powerful: force under control. We all have power and access to power and can use for different purposes and in different ways.

Here we have the Green Man, a symbol of fertility, vitality, and life force. He calms and controls the lion not through overpowering it but by accepting it. He does not try to change its nature but rather helps it to control itself. This is not to say that nature or our natural inclinations are bad. Indeed, it is the opposite. For we usually try to contain our urges and desires by a force of will, which leads to shame and repression, creating our shadow selves. These shadows may seem as if they are under control but they are not, coming out at inappropriate times or in inappropriate ways.

When we accept and value all the parts of ourselves, we then become integrated. Nothing is deemed evil and everything has its proper place and time. When the parts of ourselves that we denigrate, for example, anger, are valued, they can be channeled and used in beneficial ways. This takes great patience, courage, and strength.

> Reflection
> *The Man and the Lion are not enemies. They are friends. One is not the pet to the other, nor one is a master to the other. Together they represent the Strength that comes from life, from courage, from friendship, from power, from patience, from composure, form dedication... Together.*
> *Strength is not about brain conquering brawn, or right defeating wrong, or might defending the meek. Strength is harmony and cohesiveness between what you are and what you do.*

Keywords: strength, gentleness, patience, compassion, healing, integration, courage, heart, control, discipline, fortitude, assurance, potency, virility, lust, instinct, ability, mastery

Reversed: weakness; lack of discipline, control, or patience; overbearing, force, cowardice, fear, shyness

ᴙ IX . HERMIT ᴙ

Intellectual
The Universe
Astrological: Virgo
Element: Earth

Description: *An old man stands on a cube and holding a lantern high. He also has a staff on which two serpents are entwined as if the symbol of Hyppocrites.*

The Hermit walks his own path alone supported by the wisdom he gathered over the years, symbolized by his staff. This staff, a well-known symbol for healers, indicates that the pursuit of knowledge is for the goal of healing or becoming whole. He first heals himself and then, if called upon, uses his wisdom to guide others, never to control or harm them, following the dictate of "first, do no harm."

The light he carries illuminates his own path. He has condensed all that he has learned into a bright light that represents his own inner Divine spark. He follows no one else's and does not seek followers. As he continues his journey, he continues to seek out what is good and true so that he can add to his light, his wisdom. His own increasing light does not take away from others but instead adds to the general illumination of the world.

The Hermit represents a time of no longer listening to others, no longer seeking guidance from anyone else. It is time to withdraw and weigh all the information gathered against the only measure that matters: one's own truth. Being alone and removing all other influences is the best avenue to self-discovery. In this way, our light shines in the darkness and grows stronger. It may be that such a light attracts others, but that is not what is important. Anyone's light can be an example, but in the end, we must all light our way and heal ourselves.

Reflection
The Hermit is a seeker... gazing continuously to the Universe. The Hermit is the question, before it is the answer; it is the silence before it is the word, it is the stillness before it is the run, it is the doubt before it is the certainty. The Hermit is also the healing before it is the wound, the laugh before it is the joke, the yes before it is the "please", and the "alone" before it is the "together".

Keywords: solitude, introspection, philosophy, meditation, withdrawal, contemplation, wisdom, guidance, seeking, mysticism, privacy, prudence

Reversed: introversion, agoraphobia, ostracism, exile, paranoia, loneliness, isolation, extreme withdrawal, self-absorption, social misfit

❧ X . WHEEL ❧

Intellectual
The Unknown
Astrological: Jupiter
Element: Fire

Description: *Three women dance on a cube. One is a young girl, the second is a pregnant woman and the third is an old crone. They raise their hands to the center of a wheel.*

We are so familiar with the cycles of life, for our holidays all revolve around that idea. It is hard-wired into our psyche. But we are also creatures of our culture which, in recent decades, has focused on the idea of self-determination, of being in total control of our lives. As magick workers and diviners, we try to understand the energies at work in a situation so we can better control it.

We have forgotten some things our ancestors were very familiar with: the role of the three Fates, the role of luck and chance, and the notion that we are not God or Goddess in charge of everything. Chaos is part of the human experience yet it is in our nature to impose order on chaos.

The Wheel reminds us that we are human and not gods, that we are subject to luck and chance and fate, just like the rest of creation. Why is this so? Why do bad things happen to good people? One answer is that without challenges, we are never tested on the lessons we are learning. It is easy to be true when things go our way, but how do we react when pressed?

A turn of the Wheel can bring a windfall just as easily as a loss. The question is, how far off kilter do such events throw you? The closer to the center of the Wheel, the less you feel its effects.

Reflection
The Wheel is the cycle: Maiden, Mother and Crone ; spring, summer, fall and winter ; day and night ; happiness and loss ; understanding and doubt. But the cycle is a Wheel: Maiden, Mother and Crone and Maiden again; spring summer, fall, winter and spring again ; day, night and day again ; happiness and loss and again happiness ; understanding and doubt and a new understanding.
Never desire to stop the Wheel, even if tomorrow is unknown.

Keywords: fortune, chance, cycle of life, opportunity, destiny, fate, good luck, movement, turning point, annual event

Reversed: bad luck, out of control, misfortune, failure, unexpected setback, reversal, delay

◈ XI . JUSTICE ◈

Intellectual
The Goddess
Astrological: Libra
Element: Air

Description: *A blindfolded, pregnant woman stands on a cube. There is a dark tree on her right and a light tree on her left. She looks to her right and keeps her hands near her mouth. She blows and many leaves scatter to the wind from her hands... and in the distance they turn in colored butterflies that lighten the dark tree.*

The Justice of nature is not human justice. The black and white of her world are not judged as "right" and "wrong." They are the opposing energies of the world. She seeks not to change them or condemn them. Instead, the Justice of nature transforms dead leaves into butterflies, death into life, dark into light. Nature moves toward balance. When things become out of balance, she transform them, bringing them back into balance, helping the wheel of life continue to turn.

Keeping the balance of nature follows a simple law: all actions have consequences. But not just the external actions, for this Justice is blind and she sees with her inner eye to the inner motivations. She also sees a larger picture than any of us can hope to understand. A tree goes dormant and sheds its leaves. This is not good or bad, it part of the cycle of life. From that action, she brings new life, life that wouldn't have existed without the dead leaves.

This card indicates that whatever is going on, it is a consequence of past actions, not merely chance, as we saw in the Wheel.

> Reflection
> *Justice without mercy is like a body without a soul. Justice is a caring energy, and not a harsh unforgivable mistress. The Universe provides everything with growth, and true Justice does not punish or compensate for loss, but she turns the energies around so that everything turns to good in the Universe. But as we human cannot see ever the big picture, sometimes we need to have faith in Justice in order to be able to see it.*

Keywords: justice, karma, cause and effect, equality, truth, responsibility, integrity, fairness, judgment, contract, legal action, lawsuit, trial

Reversed: injustice, imbalance, dishonesty, hypocrisy, complications, abuse of power, red tape, bad decision

✒ XII . HANGED MAN ✒

Intellectual
Magick
Astrological: Neptune
Element: Water

Description: *A man is in a bound headstand yoga position and engulfed in a column of light.*

Traditional tarot decks depicted a man hanging upside down from a tree as a traitor. He had turned against what was the commonly accepted behaviors and values of his culture and was seen as a threat to stability. In our world, we still punish those who are a threat to the public good. However, in tarot we've moved this sort of thing to the Minor Arcana and instead focusing on the aspect of being a traitor as a spiritual act.

When not threatening limb or life of others, questioning things adds value to a society, helping it avoid stagnation and encouraging growth. This card was also connected to the idea of sacrifice and that is still true, as it does take courage and sacrifice to step outside of the normal way to living.

The Hanged Man reminds us that when we push ourselves, when explore the boundaries of what is comfortable, when you put ourselves in a position to see things from a different point of view, we have much to gain. When we give ourselves over to such an experience with perfect love and perfect trust, we are rewarded with enlightenment. If we struggle and fuss, we miss an opportunity. Relax and experience what is going on, let it infuse your body, mind, heart, and spirit. Open yourself to the wisdom to be gained.

Reflection
The Hanged Man depicts a process of acceptance, actually of changing one-self, consciously making an effort to be different, to be better. As an Archetype the reversed position indicated a powerful change of perspective obtained at a grave personal cost. But changes in the mind are more difficult that changes in the body. Changing an opinion? Listening to others? Overcoming preju-dices? Escape from habits and conventions? They are very difficult things, because they involve a painful change, or adaptation that came from letting what is around is inside.

Keywords: reversal, letting go, sacrifice, suspension, surrender, withdrawal, restriction, crisis, delay, restraint, detachment, enlightenment, transformation, initiation

Reversed: limbo, martyrdom, indecision, self-sabotage, narrow-minded, punishment, imprisonment, treason

❧ XIII . DEATH ❧

Intellectual
Energy
Astrological: Scorpio
Element: Water

Description: *No person is present; this is only a discarded robe lying on the cube. The sun is rising on the distant horizon. On one side of the cube there is a caterpillar. On the left, in the direction of the sun, there is a very beautiful monarch butterfly.*

Death, traditionally one of the "scary" cards of tarot. Even for those of us who know better, who know that "death" means "transition," when the old image of Death wielding a scythe and cutting down the living comes up, our breath catches in our throats. Even the gentle word "transition" means change and we do not usually embrace change with open arms.

Instead of sharp blades and harsh, painful endings, let us examine death from the point of view of nature, for as pagans, nature is our true bible and it is from her we should take our lessons. The caterpillar and the butterfly are an excellent symbol for the experience of death. One moment, the creature is land bound and squishy. Then, after a time of metamorphosis, it is a creature of both land and air, ethereal and free in a way it never was before, the time of change and the desires of the past forgotten.

There is a Buddhist saying, "pain is inevitable, suffering is optional." The time of metamorphosis may be painful, as change often is. Pain is a part of life. However, suffering is caused by the anxiety of trying to hold onto things that are changing. And we know that life is change. Every second of your life, you are changing. To try to fight that is insanity and is the cause of suffering. Death is change, it is not suffering.

Death is the moment when we let go of the past and embrace the future.

Reflection
One element that is difficult to see in the Death card is the emptiness. The other elements of transformation are very easy to see. The caterpillar sheds his skin (the unnecessary) and becomes a butterfly, while the sun dawning expresses a new beginning. But the rest of the card is empty.
The bigger a change is the simpler it is. Perhaps this is true because only necessity makes us really ready for big changes. And what remains is potential, a white page with no burden of luggage. Because when there is transformation what was vitally important just one minute earlier is but empty air a second later.

Keywords: death, rebirth, endings, mortality, loss, change, failure, destruction, severing ties, transitions, transformation, inexorable force, elimination

Reversed: loss of hope, decay, corruption, depression, inertia, holding on

✦ XIV . TEMPERANCE ✦

Intellectual
Balance
Astrological: Sagittarius
Element: Fire

Description: *Half of the card is in day, the other is night. In the middle there is smiling girl on a cube. She holds a cup in each hand. The daytime cup is upside down. A flower is blossoming just where she is watering. On the night side, the cup is up and a small yellow bird is drinking from it.*

Moderation in all things, or so the ancient Greeks might have us believe. Such a simple little statement and yet, when examined, it is not. And to some, it is a boring statement, for what is the fun in denying yourself? Some time in the course of history moderation turned into abstinence and denial of pleasure. But let us rid ourselves of this puritan baggage and discover what Temperance is really about.

Temperance is a fluid, changing state. It must be because its goal is to maintain balance, which is a state that does not deny pleasure but maintains life so that pleasure may be enjoy to its fullest. Maintaining balance is not a matter of strict divisions all the time. It is knowing when to give and when to take as well as how much. Nature, again our best bible, shows us that perfectly equal balance only occurs twice a year at the equinoxes. Timing is everything.

Temperance is also about blending, again not equal parts of everything all the time, but knowing when, what, and how much is needed to create that wonderful alchemy where all things are in balance for that moment. Being temperate means being aware of all the energies present working with them all in harmony with an eye toward both the moment and the bigger picture. It is truly an act of magick.

Reflection
Temperance also represents the connection between give and take, wait and do, listen and say. If our daily life is seen as an exchange of energies, we must be careful not to be overly aggressive (give too much, talk too much, decide too much, force too much...) and not to be overly receptive (accept too much, listen too much, follow too much, bend too much). We need to take space in our lives, and that space should be no bigger nor smaller than ourselves.

Keywords: temperance, self-control, balance, moderation, harmony, synthesis, patience, health, combination, blending, management, unification, synthesis, synergy, guides, angels

Reversed: imbalance, excess, temper, one-sided relationship, irreconcilable differences, short term focus

⚘ XV . DEVIL ⚘

Spiritual
Unknown
Astrological: Capricorn
Element: Earth

Description: *Suspended over a cube of light, there is a mirror. A dead tree is reflected in the mirror. Outside of the mirror is day, inside the mirror is night. Two chains hang from the mirror frame.*

The Devil is complicated. The Devil is the dark side…of life and of ourselves. It is Prometheus, the snake who invites us to learn about good and evil, the Fallen Angel, the Id. It is Thanatos and Eros united. It is the reminder of our untamed, instinctual selves and a gateway to the spiritual, to a new kind of magickian. All of this sounds very exciting and seductive, and it is. And if misunderstood, can be dangerous, to ourselves, each other, and out planet.

We look at the Devil and we see something, probably something we dislike or are afraid of. We don't realize that the Devil is a mirror, reflecting back only what we project onto it. But it is a special mirror that shows our shadows, not our carefully crafted masks that we normally show ourselves and the world.

The thirst for life, the fear of and fascination with death, the drive of lust, the desire for pleasure, animal instincts, these powerful impulses live in all of us. Prometheus gave us fire, the ability to control light. The snake, the gift of free will. These things make us human and different from the rest of nature. We are of nature and apart from nature and this struggle is at the root of the Devil. Where do our desires end and we begin? What do we cling to and what do we free ourselves from? Only by examining these things can we truly free ourselves and understand who we really are, which is the great work of magickal and spiritual growth.

Reflection
The Devil is the first card among those in the Spiritual Sphere. In many ways he acts like a Guardian of the Threshold. He represents our dark side. And as any mirror it only has the power we allow it. But it has power. A lot of power, because it is in our nature to have a dark side. And that side chains us to the bottom, even when we try to go to the sky. Sometimes the Devil is fear, sometimes is greed, sometimes is childishness, sometimes is blindness... he changes shapes to fit the challenge we need to overcome in that moment. But there is only one common thing among the many shapes of the Devil: it does not bring any life.

Keywords: bondage, obsession, materialism, temptation, shadow, fear, doubt, lies, violence, deviancy, ignorance, sexuality, hopelessness, lack of options, trapped, scape goat

Reversed: abuse, addiction, violence, evil, weakness, detachment, breaking free, reclaiming power

❧ XVI . TOWER ❧

Spiritual
Energy
Astrological: Mars
Element: Fire

Description: *Behind a cube and standing tall there is a beautiful tree. On a branch there is a bird's nest and a bird remaining in it. Another bird is flying away as lightning threatens.*

The birds have spent time finding just the right home and building just the right nest. They've become comfortable and feel safe. At least they did until the storm hit. We don't see the lightning actually hitting the tree, but the birds know it is just a matter of time. Once it is destroyed, their home will never be the same again. They have to take with them whatever they can, maybe a prized bit of fluff, and rebuild.

And so it is with us. We spent time and energy, investing emotionally in the structures of our lives. We create homes for our personal lives, our work. We build carefully crafted belief structures and relationships. We come to depend on and love them. We get to the point where we cannot imagine our lives without them.

As noted earlier, in the Wheel and in Death, humans resist change, even when the things we cling to are no longer good for us. The house no longer suits. The job no longer challenges. The relationship no longer satisfies. The belief system holds us back. And so we stay put. Until we can't. Sometimes the Universe, in its benevolent wisdom, forces a change. Sometimes the thing just falls apart. And suddenly we are free. Free to examine the rubble that remains, deciding what is too damaged to bother with, what needs to be left behind, and what treasures to bring along to add to the new structure.

> Reflection
> *The Tower is the connection between the healing energy and the destructive energy. In some ways, it is about the necessity of pain.*
> *Nature is full of pain. Through human eyes, sometimes nature is cruel. But where the body and the mind recognize pain and are afraid of it, the soul sees pain as an experience. It is very difficult to understand, or even to accept it, but the Tower energy is a friend, even if it brings pain.*

Keywords: sudden change, upheaval, adversity, downfall, destruction, catastrophe, misery, disaster, ruin, chaos, release, awakening, freedom, escape

Reversed: fear of change, prolonged upheaval, obstacles, difficulties, losses, oppression, imprisonment, tyranny

≈ XVII . STARS ≈

Spiritual
Magick
Astrological: Aquarius
Element: Air

Description: *In the starry night the evanescent figure of the God and the Goddess are touching their fingers as in the Michelangelo's Sistine chapel.*

The Star is such a lovely card. Here the Goddess and God touch and at the point of Their intersection, a star appears. We understand that the Divine is unknowable and we understand that the Goddess and God are really the Divine revealed as opposites so that we may know Them and It at least on some level. We do not value one over the other, but love and value Them both. Together they create the Divine, our North Star, by which we sail the ship of our souls.

Stars play many roles, both mythic and mundane, in the lives of humans. As noted, we use them for navigation, mundane and spiritual. We like to wish upon a star, trusting our hopes and dreams to their tender care. Looking at the stars gives us perspective, reminding us that we, too, are made of the same stuff as these brilliant pieces of light in the darkness. The constellations tell stories. We use them to find understanding, direction, and hope. Their gentle yet brilliant light gives comforting hope in times of darkness. They are not illusionary like the moon nor overwhelming like the sun. They are soft, gentle, and yet amazingly powerful.

The Star represents refreshment and cleansing after trouble. It promises restored faith and renewed purpose when we are at our most vulnerable. As we pour our faith and trust into the world, we receive healing and guidance through the constant universal flow of the Divine.

Reflection
If we look at the Infinite, the Infinite will look into us. Magick is a miracle. And miracles happen everyday if we can recognize them.

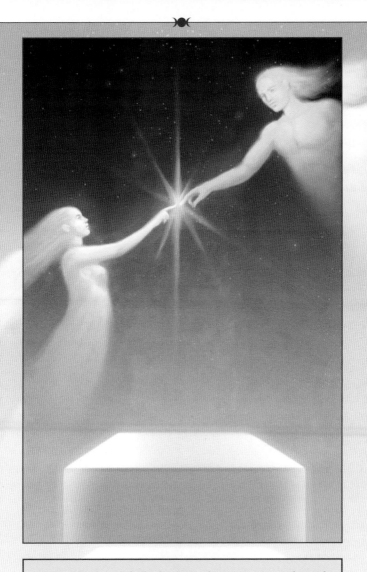

Keywords: hope, faith, healing, cleansing, renewal, guidance, peace, blessing, tranquility, serenity, inspiration, optimism, happiness, promises, wishes

Reversed: lack of faith, hopelessness, discouragement, feeling lost, broken dreams, dashed hopes, unfulfilled wishes, missed opportunities

Spiritual
The Goddess
Astrological: Pisces
Element: Water

Description: *A full Moon is shining in the sky. A woman is standing raising her arms toward the moon. She has a pendant with the triple moon on her neck. She is dressed like the High Priestess.*

While the Empress is, in tarot, the Goddess on earth and of the material realm, this is the Goddess of the heavens and of the spiritual realm. The material realm and spiritual realm are not separate but as humans, we comprehend facets better than the whole, at least for a while. So here is the Queen of the Night, changeable, mysterious, and beguiling. She governs our dreams and speaks to our deepest intuitive selves.

It is a wonder that more people don't associate the Goddess of the moon with the Trickster, for She is not above illusions and tricks. At least what She shows us may seem like tricks. One minute something appears as a monster in the corner and the next, it is just a duffle bag we left on the floor. She reminds us that everything is not as it seems. We should take nothing at face value. Instead, we need to look with our spiritual eyes as well as our physical eyes. There is a world that exists alongside and within our material reality. If we spend enough time in her presence, our eyes grow accustomed to this different kind of light. We see less, we see more, we see differently.

She brings us visions and dreams. She gifts us with psychic abilities. She asks us to pay attention to our intuition, to tease out the secrets of the world, to become comfortable with uncertainty. The world by moonlight is a different place than the world by day. The reality created by the light of the Moon isn't less real than the world by sunlight. So often we forget that and miss out on half of the wonders of life.

Reflection
The Light of the Moon changes what she touches. She does not actually change its nature, but she changes our perception, revealing the hidden things. The Moon turns truth to opinion, changes certainty to doubt, and answers to questions. The Moon transforms stagnant water into river and seas, takes what is simple it makes deep, surround what is known with the haze of the "maybe."

Keywords: secrets, illusion, deception, imagination, mystery, subconscious, confusion, falsehoods, cycles, bewilderment, anxiety, insecurity, dreams, nightmares, visions, psychic ability

Reversed: secrets revealed, mysteries unveiled, insomnia, trouble sleeping, irrationality, shadows, danger

❧ XIX . SUN ❧

Spiritual
The God
Astrological: Sun
Element: Fire

Description: *The Sun is shining at his zenith. A man is standing, raising his arms to the sun. He has a pendant with the sun on his neck. He is dressed like the High Priest.*

The Emperor is the God of the material realm. The Sun is the God of the spiritual realm, although as mentioned in the Moon, these two realms, in reality, are one. The God of the Sun governs our purest intellect, our clear understanding of spiritual precepts. Through his gifts, we acquire knowledge, we practice discernment, we communicate and share our wisdom.

Our society values intellect and rational thought at the expense of intuition and psychic abilities. For us, those who walk the pagan path, we have learned to value the intuitive and the psychic within us and sometimes push the pendulum too far and reject the intellect. This turns the intellect into a shadow. The Sun reminds us that all facets of our human means of experiencing the world have value, including our conscious mind and all its glorious abilities.

By the light of the Sun, we can see clearly and make sense of the world. By the light of the Sun, the world comes alive. The Sun gives us energy, vitality, and joy. Together with the Moon, this card forms a complete day, the fullness of time in which we live, grow, learn, and celebrate.

Reflection
The Light of the Sun illuminates what he touches. It does not actually enhance its nature, but he allows us to focus our perception, bringing attention to everything. The Sun changes opinions into truths, changes doubt into certainty and questions to answers. The Sun transform a lump of land into a beautiful landscape, what is complicated it is made simple, and what is clouded is finally made clear.

Keywords: happiness, joy, fun, optimism, enthusiasm, glory, clarity, consciousness, success, celebration, energy, vitality, good fortune, greatness, life

Reversed: ego, false impressions, delayed happiness, depression, burnt out, over exposure, drought, partial success, incomplete victory

✵ XX . JUDGEMENT ✵

Spiritual
The Universe
Astrological: Pluto
Element: Fire

Description: *There are six stars one exactly under the other in the center of the card, connected by a ray of light. A bird flies in the sky. Around the ray of light there is an ascending energy that spiral upwards, made of many spirits.*

We are all on a path seeking our highest spiritual evolution. It is mostly a gentle slope, with small lessons being learned each day. Every once in a while, though, we have a burst of growth. Something within us resonates to some call that seems both outside of us but also inside of us at the same time. We hear it, feel it, and we recognize it as truth and realize it is a call to something new, something bigger and better than what we before. As we listen to it, as we try to decipher its guidance, it grows stronger, as our spirit and the Divine begin to dance together, traveling up through our chakras, waking us up.

Maybe the call scares us, asks too much of us, and we ignore it. That may work for a time, but not for long, because our spirits yearn to be born, desire to find expression in this world. The pure truth of it settles into our lower chakra, perhaps causing discomfort until we act, perhaps quelling fears so we can jump up and accept the challenge. And so it moves up, up, up, from the basest of matter to the most ethereal of spirit within us until it accepted, embraced, and owned.

This spiritual drive fills us until it must break free and be expressed in the world. And then, ironically, this most ethereal of impulses becomes material as it is manifest in our lives and consequently in the world. We have just taken a huge leap in our spiritual growth. This is the Judgement card. There is nothing of judgement in it, just an invitation to discover and be your truest self.

Reflection
There are 7 major chakras, but only 6 are portrayed. As the Chakras, and also the Tree of Life, express the connection between the material and the Divine as a road, suggesting that Illumination is the purpose of human existence. But even if there is no Illumination, and no grand desire to be a "Saint" of this or that belief... we cannot deny the connection between the Self and the Universe, and between the Universe and the Self.

Keywords: rebirth, renewal, rite of passage, calling, vocation, awakening, change, decision, forgiveness, redemption, absolution, judgment

Reversed: doubt, forsaking vocation, ignoring a calling, avoiding change, unhealed wounds, lack of forgiveness, delay

✧ XXI . THE WORLD ✧

Spiritual
Balance
Astrological: Saturn
Element: Earth

Description: *An ancient tree grows from the cube. A small young tree is growing on the side. An old woman holds the hand of a young boy.*

The ancient tree, the young sapling. The old woman, the young boy. Beginnings and endings. The World card tells the story of great achievements. It also tells a secret about these achievements: there is no end of the story, not really. A tree lives for decades, maybe centuries, a glorious life through so many seasons, before it dies. After it is gone, after its shadow is no more, the sapling that grew from its seed flourishes and begins its own story, similar to the old one but unique as well. A woman lives, learning to love and forgive and share, watching her children grow and their children grow. She leaves them her legacy, in the genes she has passed on, in the traditions she's created, in the life lessons she's shared. These children and children's children bring something of her into the future, along with their own unique spirits and lives.

With the World card, we find that we've reached an ending of sorts, something that can be marked, at any rate, in our human way. Graduating. Getting a new job. Joining another in marriage. These milestones mark endings for us, achievements of which we can be proud. But our journey doesn't end with them, only pauses for a moment of sweet celebration, before continuing on.

Reflection
All in one, one in all. Balance is natural: harmonious. It may seem a small thing, but balance and harmony are really the same. It's true that you experience balance in your soul when the constant conflict between different things is solved naturally, because of what it is, and of what you are, rather then because of choices, negotiations, and sacrifices.

Keywords: completion, success, perfection, achievement, accomplishment, victory, reward, unity, wholeness, fulfillment, endings and beginnings, celebration, center of attention, travel

Reversed: delays, hesitations, false starts, stagnation, rut, incomplete work, lack of closure

ZERO . THE FOOL

Astrological: Uranus
Element: Air

Description: *Overhead, the sun and the moon in a partial eclipse. A lonely tree stands in the distance in an empty field. A path leads directly to the tree.*

The Fool is the space in between and it is the space where everything exists. It is both night and day and also neither. Nothing and everything coexist at the same time, in all time, in the now, which is the only time. It is the silence before the sound. The Fool is a conundrum, a riddle without an answer until one is given.

For us, for our lives, we are the Fool when we are at a point where anything, or almost anything, is possible. Until we make a choice and in choosing are immediately no longer in this space. But before that decision is made, all possibilities exist. There are no good and bad or right and wrong. Everything just is.

You are here, now, in this empty place filled with everything that can ever be. You get to fill this space with whatever you wish. The path doesn't exist until you take your first step and then a next. With each step, the path takes shape, gains definition. Soon you will be running along that path and it will be night or it will be day, but not both. You won't know until you move. You are the center of this world and it is your choice that will create it. Make your choice, make the leap. Start your new journey and see what wonderful things come of it.

Reflection
The Fool is the beginning and the end. And it is everything in between. It is that... and it is not.
Maybe the real key to understand the Fool is to see is for what it "is not,"
Define the Fool by what it is not... it is the zero, it's empty, and you need to fill it with your own meaning, but it will still be empty... with the same clarity as the present becomes the past and the future became the present.

Keywords: beginnings, innocence, freedom, spontaneity, adventure, youth, idealism, faith, purity, fearlessness, carelessness, eccentricity, apparent foolishness

Reversed: folly, foolishness, carelessness, stupidity, negligence, distraction, naivety, recklessness, risk-taking

CHAPTER 5:
THE MINOR ARCANA

While the Major Arcana cards of the Major Arcana represent important themes in our lives, the Minor Arcana cards illustrate the everyday events of our lives. We find the themes of the Major cards woven throughout our lives in the simple actions of daily life. These cards help us pinpoint the precise areas in our lives where these major themes are expressing themselves. Combining both the Major and Minor cards, we can identify patterns and find answers to help us live with passion, love, discernment, and wisdom.

For each card, you will find the card title, the Silver Witchcraft name, the suit meaning, the number meaning, the traditional meaning, the season, a short description of the image followed by a more in-depth meaning, and keywords for the cards in both their upright and reversed positions.

Witchcraft and magick are connected to seasons and cycles. Witches learn to recognize and work in cooperation with the energies of the earth. The Silver Witchcraft Tarot incorporates this energetic dance into its images and meanings. In each suit, the cards numbered two through nine move through the seasons, with the twos starting in Winter (marked by Yule) and ending in Autumn (Samhain). In this way, we follow the suit's essence from its seed in the Ace through its lifespan during a year and ending with the fullness of the suit in the ten.

The seasonal associations can be used to determine timing when seeking predictions. However, it is important to remember to not only interpret these connections literally. Almost everything in tarot can be read as metaphors. So the seasons may not necessarily relate to literal seasons, but to phases of a situation. A new job or new relationship can occur in winter but metaphorically, it is represented by the springtime. Conversely, a project or partnership can end in summer but would show up in the cards as late autumn, a symbolic time of endings. Keep this in mind as you read the interpretations and apply them to your own readings.

Agriculture, the planting, tending, harvesting, and storing of plants for sustenance, plays a huge role in pagan beliefs. While most of us no longer grow our own food, we still rely on these cycles and use them as metaphors for all aspects of our lives. When we speak of tending the tender seedlings, for example, we don't necessarily mean food or plants. This represents anything we've begun in our lives, whether it is a new relationship, a creative project, or educational pursuit.

Once you begin reading the cycles of the year and theme of agriculture as metaphor, you can easily extrapolate the cards meanings to any situation you are using the cards to explore.

> Cycles, experience and everyday life
> *The theme of "Cycles" is very important when using Tarot. In modern cultures, we often suffer the simplification that moving through life is moving along a line, from a beginning to an end.*
>
> *It's like watching a movie knowing that there will be a happy ending and all the narrative themes will be wrapped up. Life, however, is more complicated that this. To each end there is a beginning, to each beginning an end. And everything flows.*
>
> *Cycles in life… growing, enjoying, collecting, resting and growing again… are like breathing. You need all parts to be healthy. You need winter as much as summer. And they are connected one to the other.*

The connections between numerals and seasons in the deck is used to remind of this constant flow of experiences in every situation and in every person. Many times, it could be wiser asking the Tarot not "what will happen," but "in what part of the cycle I am." So, if you are in winter, gather your strength. In Autumn, collect your resources. In Spring, give energies to new beginning. In Summer, live the moment before it passes on.

≈ THE SUIT OF CHALICES ≈

Chalices are linked to the endless mystery of feeling and emotions.

If you think about yourself, the Chalices express the part of you that you will never understand, but that you just "know." Emotions are meant to flow… express, come and go, and move endlessy, sometimes keeping the same through years, even if they change in the surface.

In the Silver Withcraft deck, the Chalics are symbolized by Silvery Moons. The Moon is an expression of the constant change of the emotions. Like seasons, the Moon goes through a cycle of herself, always powerful, even when hidden. She calls to us, and sometimes we call to her: remember that emotions are not meant to be understood or controlled, but they can be recognized, welcomed or let go.

⚶ ACE OF CHALICES ⚶

A tide in the harmony of the Soul

Suit meaning: mysteries, feelings and emotions
Number meaning: the source of emotions
Traditional meaning: the source of water/redemption
Season: none
Description: the moon is reflected in a chalice that is pouring water.

The Goddess, as symbolized by the Moon, is the source of love, grace, healing, and redemption. The Moon represents emotions, which shape our relationships. Just as the moon waxes and wanes and just as tides ebb and flow, so do our feelings. The Ace, though, is an outpouring from the Goddess to us and then from us to the people in our lives. This is an opportunity to let the essence and the promise of the Goddess fill the chalices of our souls and renew our hearts. The Ace of Cups is an invitation to drink deeply from the love of the Goddess and find healing, redemption, and love. Once refreshed, we can more easily share and attract the love, peace, and healing we all desire. As a situation, it indicates a new beginning or fresh start. As advice, it suggests forgiveness and healing.

The deepest emotions are something Sacred. All emotions we feel may have different sources. But the deepest ones, they are a connection to the Divine. As such, we should consider human spirit like a temple, and always thread carefully on it, be it our soul or that of somebody else.

Keywords: relationship, peace, love, healing, grace, creativity, joy, overwhelming emotions, intuition, affection
Reversed: separation, resentment, bitterness, stagnation, lack of connection, rejection of Spirit, a missed opportunity

≈ TWO OF CHALICES ≈

The hands of love

Suit meaning: mysteries, feelings and emotions
Number meaning: Yule/Winter solstice—a safe world
Traditional meaning: a marriage, pact or partnership
Season: Winter
Description: a man and a woman, in ritual robes, are holding hand to hand. The other hand is raised to the sky and the moon shines over them.

Under the pale light of the moon shines one snow-covered world. Life and love seem like a distant memory as we approach the longest night of the year and the light seems so weak and far away. Yet, just as we move through that long, dark night, we do so with the faith that the light will come again. We celebrate that night and welcome the returning light. That tiny increase in daylight fuels our faith. And so it is when we look into the eyes of someone and recognize a kindred connection. We recognize the potential and with great faith, we make our promises. The seed of the Ace has been planted and we vow to nurture it and see what grows, even though we may not have evidence of bounty for some time. But it is too early to worry about the future. For now, we reach out and grasp the hand of love and are willing to explore the mystery of this miraculous connection with another.

> *Sharing emotions is the most important act of love. Emotions became a link with a person you love (not necessarily a partner, but maybe just a friend, or a family member) and creates a connection that extends to all the Universe. There is no difference between love and Love, because they merge together when you look at the Universe.*

Keywords: union, partnership, connection, falling in love at first sight, harmony, love, feeling in love, kindred spirit, attraction, romance
Reversed: discord, argument, unrequited love, repulsion, rejection, rose-colored glasses

❧ THREE OF CHALICES ❧

The morning dance

Suit meaning: mysteries, feelings and emotions
Number meaning: Imbolc — the world awakens
Traditional meaning: a happy celebration
Season: Winter giving way to Spring
Description: three females, the maiden, the mother, and the crone, are dancing under the moon

Faith is paying off, as the first signs of spring begin to appear. As the story goes, Demeter brings forth the first flowers of the season to welcome her daughter, Persephone, back from the Underworld. When mother and daughter reunite after some many months, there is great joy and celebration as they greet each other. The world joins in, dancing and praising the Goddess. After living so long in the dark and the cold, even a little light and warmth and new life are reason enough to celebrate. The 3 of Chalices describes a situation that includes celebrating for any reason, big or small, but mostly appreciating the presence of people in our lives. As advice, it reminds us to express our happy feelings and to enjoy the simple things in life with those we love most.

> *Inner emotions should not stay hidden. Smile, laugh, dance, cry, sing, giggle… Let the emotions go outward and inward with every breath. Live with spontaneity and the Universe will join your dance. Just remember that there is not a wrong moment to be yourself, maiden, mother or crone that you are.*

Keywords: friendship, family, casual parties, joy, fun, abandon, abundance, celebration, connections, savoring the moment
Reversed: excessive partying, the morning after, awkward situations, feeling left out

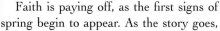

✤ FOUR OF CHALICES ✤

The eye of the joyful storm

Suit meaning: mysteries, feelings and emotions

Number meaning: Ostara/Spring equinox—a moment full of energy

Traditional meaning: boredom

Season: Spring

Description: A woman in ritual robe rest asleep under the moon, leaning against a tree, while many rabbits and small animals scuttle around her.

The Spring equinox is a time of equal parts light and dark. It is a pivotal moment just before the time of light in a day becomes longer than the night. There is this intake of breath, this calm before the world explodes with burgeoning life. The 4 of Chalices explores that contradictory human state when we have the beauty of life opening before us and yet we feel bored or dissatisfied. This card asks us to reflect on what we find so attractive that it causes us to neglect the gifts under our nose. Perhaps it is that strange human ability to project into the future. We know that life is approaching a pinnacle and instead of enjoying it, we begin to worry about what will happen after it passes. Spring has hardly begun and we are worried about the hard work of harvesting or the lack of winter. This card describes a situation of ignoring life's wonders. The advice is easy: look around and enjoy all that life has to offer.

> *Sometimes you don't need to have strong emotions to live in the world. As we are not unconnected, the drive and the energy can came from outside. If all the joy and all the life in the Universe were a storm, you would want to be in the center of it: a quiet spot, surrounded by contagious life.*

Keywords: discontent, dissatisfaction, ennui, boredom, lack of gratitude, depression, resisting change, stagnation, lack of inspiration

Reversed: deeper depression, unhealthy or dangerous responses to boredom, taking pleasure in wallowing

⚖ FIVE OF CHALICES ⚖

Giving and taking

Suit meaning: mysteries, feelings and emotions

Number meaning: Beltane—a world growing and connecting

Traditional meaning: partial loss

Season: Spring giving to Summer

Description: under a moon, a woman in ritual robe has blown out 3 candles of different colors. A white and a pink candle are still burning brightly, under the light of the moon.

For many, the focus Beltane, or May Day, is life and sexuality. It is also a time, like Samhain, when the veil between the worlds is thin. We may experience communication for loved ones who have passed, a bittersweet experience of happy connection but also of remembrance and longing. During this time, plants are growing but are still tenuous and in need of great care. In fact, in order to assure that plants grow strong and healthy, seedlings have to thinned. It can be hard deciding what tender shoots to pull out for the benefit of the rest. In this card, the 5 of Chalices, we see a woman selecting which candles to extinguish and which to leave burning. It is a time of give and take, of making decisions about what will survive and hopefully thrive into the future and what must be killed. We mourn the loss of what must go even while we continue to nurture that which remains.

> *To take you have to give. To give you have to take. Balance is not a paycheck with figures, but you must keep the flow of energy going in both directions. Every transition, every choice, brings with it loss and gain together. They are part of the same whole, and as a whole, you must accept them, without regret, but as part of the natural life.*

Keywords: mourning, feelings of loss, sadness, regret, repentance, bitterness, frustration, difficult choices

Reversed: self-pity, obsessing over the past, beating yourself up, failure to mourn

≈ SIX OF CHALICES ≈

The garden of plenty

Suit meaning: mysteries, feelings and emotions
Number meaning: Litha/Summer solstice — an explosion of beauty
Traditional meaning: memory
Season: Summer
Description: Two children play under the Moon, into a rock garden, full of new blossoms and flowers.

Halcyon weather is calm, peaceful and tranquil. Halcyon times are characterized by wealth and prosperity. We speak fondly of the halcyon days of our youth as being happy, joyful and carefree. All of these ideas perfectly capture the essence of the 6 of Chalices and the celebration of Litha, the longest day of the year. The scarcity of winter forgotten, there is plenty to be had and the promise of even more to come. The God is at his strongest and the Goddess smiles down upon all creation. It is as if light and abundance fill the world so full of good things that there is no space or time for worry or sadness. We are bloated with happy memories, plans for good times, and no concerns for the future. We feel open and generous. Life is good and there is no threat in sight.

> *Some moments are just to be enjoyed. No future. No past. Just the present. To be yourself, you won't need to be always the same. To say "I love you" you don't need to love "forever," as long as you love "now" truly. The present moment, as fleeting as it may be, is your center.*

Keywords: nostalgia, happy memories, kindness, innocence, selflessness, generosity, innocent pleasures, unconditional affection
Reversed: living in or romanticizing the past, insincere actions, manipulation, buying affection or friendship

≈ SEVEN OF CHALICES ≈

The harvest of the heart

Suit meaning: mysteries, feelings and emotions
Number meaning: Lammas—the harvest in the world
Traditional meaning: fantasy
Season: Summer giving way to Autumn
Description: A woman in a ritual robe harvests 7 different "fruits," under the moon. There is honey, grapes (green and purple), tomatoes, pears, apples and corn.

There are so many good things in the world, so many opportunities and options, and it feels like time is running out! That's how Lammas sometimes feels. The first big harvests are ready to be brought in and the days are starting to be noticeably shorter. This card, the 7 of Chalices, illustrates a time in our lives when we have so many choices and we aren't sure which to pick. Our focus is scattered and we don't really want to decide; we want it all! We are feeling so greedy that even things that we don't really want or might not be good for us beg for attention, stretching our limited time and energy even further. It is definitely a time of an embarrassment of riches. Good advice would be to weigh your options, check in with your heart to determine what you really want, and prioritize your time and resources.

> *Your heart must be prepared to take things in. Emotions, memories, words and gestures, they all contribute to create a space into your heart. Let it be a joyous burden, even if winter is coming and things are going to pass, they will stay with you, if you treasure them carefully.*

Keywords: confusion, fantasies, choices, imagination, dreams, illusions, lack of focus, wishful thinking
Reversed: fears, daydreams interfering with responsibilities, escapism

≈ EIGHT OF CHALICES ≈

The evening tide

Suit meaning: mysteries, feelings and emotions
Number meaning: Mabon/autumn equinox—a world preparing to go to sleep
Traditional meaning: retreat
Season: Autumn
Description: A woman in ritual robe is tucking the bed of her child, around a campfire under the moon.

Here is another equinox, where daylight and dark are perfectly balanced. But instead of waking up, the world's thoughts turn to winding down. Bounty abounds and there is still work to do but we are beginning to tire. This is a good time to rest and retreat for a bit as we welcome the cooler, calmer air of autumn. As we settle down, we reflect on the past weeks and months, on everything we've invested in emotionally. Are things going as we'd hoped? Is this really the direction we want to go? Like the woman in the image, we want the best for the relationships and projects we brought forth lately. In the quiet moment when the world is held in balance, we find that we may have to prune some things and divert more energy to others.

Remember to care. To care not just for yourself, but for the Universe whole.
For others, for small and big things. Take care of them, gently, and the
Universe will take care of you. Not, maybe, in the way you are thinking,
because the Universe is much wiser than you, but you will never be alone.

Keywords: reflection, retreat, quest, journey, search, discontent, dissatisfaction, unhappiness, mission
Reversed: settling, accepting second best, running away, making excuses

❧ NINE OF CHALICES ❧

The inner door

Suit meaning: mysteries, feelings and emotions
Number meaning: Samhain — a world asleep and open spiritual doors
Traditional meaning: satisfaction
Season: Autumn giving way to Winter
Description: A woman in ritual robe sitting cross-legged under the moon and raising her hands to the sky. She has closed eyes, and it's beginning to snow.

The Nine of Chalices shows the cycle of the year ending and indicates the end of cycle in life. This is the culmination of all the work of the year and a time to give thanks and ask blessings for the coming winter. Even as the snow begins to fall and nature loses its vibrancy, we remember that bounty and powerful energy. As with Ostara, the veil between the worlds is thin and we are reminded that all that we've enjoyed, all that we've manifested on earth, began in spirit. In the hustle and bustle of bringing in the harvest, our focus has been on the physical. This is a time to not only enjoy the gifts we have received and helped create, it is a time to reconnect with the spiritual world, our ancestors, our guides and allies, and the Goddess and God.

> *Try to find a balance between the visible and the invisible, the deep and the obvious. They are not really that different or enemies one to the other. Let the door of your heart open and explore further than what you already know. The Universe is much bigger than you can imagine, and it is possible to journey even standing always in the same place.*

Keywords: wishes fulfilled, contentment, satisfaction with life, pride, hospitality, sensuality, worldly pleasures, happiness
Reversed: overindulgence, smugness, dissatisfaction, resting on laurels, selfishness

✎ TEN OF CHALICES ✎

As above, so below

Suit meaning: mysteries, feelings and emotions
Number meaning: the greater world
Traditional meaning: happiness
Description: A woman, a man and two children are standing in water. A moon and a rainbow fill the sky. The same Moon and Rainbow is mirrored in the water, behind them.

The 10 of Chalices is the full expression of the promise of the Ace of Chalices. The seed of love that was given, received, and nurtured through all the cards in between has grown, bloomed, and born fruit. What began as above, the perfect love and perfect trust from the Goddess and God, has manifested in the physical world. This is the completion of the phrase "As above, so below." As such, this card indicates deep connections and emotional intimacy. It is the kind of love that expands when it is shared. By letting the love of the Goddess into our hearts, we take the first step in allowing that love to manifest within our souls and to flow through our most important relationships. Then we have the happy experience of seeing how it moves out into the world, begetting even more love.

To love yourself, you must learn to love someone. To love someone you must learn to love. To love, it means to love the Universe.

Keywords: family, domestic bliss, optimism, comfort, tranquility, peace, sanctuary, joy, happiness, deep affection
Reversed: family disputes, arguments, unhappiness, false front, separation, broken promises, betrayal

❧ THE SUIT OF PENTACLES ❧

While we strive to fight off the pressure of modern life and her merciless soulless intent to make humans think only of material things, we begin to see a big difference between matter and spirit. But that is as much as a delusion as to think that spirit is not important. In the Suits, Pentacles express matter and materiality. And for this reason, too often the suit is discounted and taken for granted as we put more emphasis on the realms of emotions, passions and words. Mere things seems… they seem heavy, and slow, and unimportant.

In truth, the Pentacles express the link and connection between things. Nothing can really be whole unless it is given manifestation, a body. Food must be eaten and savored, a body must rest, love must be made. We must be born, we must age and, finally, we must die.

This is why in the Silver Witchcraft Tarot matter is symbolized by silver threads. Matter connects, matter makes whole, matter is just another form of energy. In a gesture, Pentacles would be the motion. In a shape, Pentacles would be the form. Not a paralyzed force and not a shade without color of the spiritual world.

In Pentacles, it's important to think about threads, connections, grounding, roots, manifestations: everything is one, and the relation between one and everything, and between everything and one. You cannot separate the Universe.

~ ACE OF PENTACLES ~

The thread that links everything

Suit meaning: coherence, stability, life, harmony
Number meaning: the source of your life energy
Traditional meaning: the source of earth/materiality
Description: an old trunk, amid vegetations and flower, where luminous gossamer threads envelop a pentacle. The threads create a triple moon design.

Our physical world is connected to the spiritual world. It is, indeed, a manifestation of spirit and it is, for as long as we inhabit our bodies, our home. The threads we weave, whether through intentional magickal practices or through our thoughts, words, and actions, are magick. They work with the energies of the universe to create our experience. The Ace of Pentacles shows the point where spirit becomes material, where what we intend becomes real. It is the tree that connects the worlds and by connecting to it, we have access to all the creativity in the universe. We are artists working with spirit and this card promises that we have the ability and the opportunity to create something worthwhile.

Everything is connected. Even when you look at material things, do not lose sight of the Divine. All things, small or big, matter.

Keywords: abundance, resources, money, wealth, health, comfort, pleasure, creation, luck, achieving goals
Reversed: lack, lost resources, physical concerns, seeking money for its own sake, a missed opportunity

✢ TWO OF PENTACLES ✢

The still dancer

Suit meaning: coherence, stability, life, harmony
Number meaning: Yule/Winter solstice—a world safe
Traditional meaning: the eternal motion
Season: Winter
Description: a woman is standing in the snow under a tree and looking at the stars. She is juggling two pentacles connected by gossamer threads. At her feet a bunny is all shrinking because of the cold, staying just next to her leg.

The Winter Solstice, our longest night, marks a turning, from darkness to light. However, for our ancestors, it also marked the continuation of a time of scarcity. Even though the light is returning, it will be a long while before more food can be grown. In the 2 of Pentacles we see that need for balance, a delicate juggling act. There is only so much to go around, at least for now. We can make it stretch but we need to be careful and prioritize. The promise of future fruitfulness is present, like the shivering bunny, but before it can grow, it must first survive.

> *It is possible to move while standing still, and to stay still while moving. Movement and pause, light and darkness, voice and silence, are all but two sides of the same coin.*

Keywords: multi-tasking, balance, tight budget, comparison-shopping, allocating resources, calm or Zen-like behavior in face of crisis
Reversed: robbing Peter to pay Paul, financial distress, awkward situation, stress, frenetic energy

⊸≋ THREE OF PENTACLES ≋⊸

Mirror of the Universe

Suit meaning: coherence, stability, life, harmony

Number meaning: Imbolc—a world awakening

Traditional meaning: a work of art

Season: Winter giving way to Spring

Description: A man is sitting in the snow, while a woman in sculpting a statue of him in an old trunk. A single crocus is blooming out of the snow with a bunny near it. Gossamer threads connect everyone… the man, the woman, the sculpture, the flower, and the pentacle.

Like the waking of the world at Imbolc, our creativity also awakens. While things may have appeared dormant on the outside, our spirits have been turned inward, processing, reflecting, being fed. Now we are beginning to turn outward, trying our hands at things that have lived only in our hearts and minds. We channel those visions, those intentions through our plans and through our hands and soon they manifest in the physical world. What seemed dead begins to show, ever so slowly, signs of life. These small signs of progress give us the inspiration we need to continue on, to commit to the long haul.

> *Every thing we do or create does not belong to us only. The inspiration came from the Universe and when we create something we are returning it to the Universe. And into the Universe it will grow and became something greater.*

Keywords: teamwork, creation, skilled work, making something of value, contributing to a worthwhile project, highlighting abilities

Reversed: ineffectual design by committee, shoddy work, not pulling your weight, not doing your best, contributions ignored

≈◎ FOUR OF PENTACLES ◎≈

Life: breathing

Suit meaning: coherence, stability, life, harmony
Number meaning: Ostara/Spring equinox—a moment full of energy
Traditional meaning: greed, limitations
Season: Spring
Description: A woman sits in the lotus yoga position, with a magickal calm upon her and eyes closed. A pentacle is in front of her. Behind her there is a bush. A bunny rushes to the bush from the left and many multicolored birds came out of the bush on the right. Gossamer threads connect everything.

Although the Spring Equinox is a time of new life, it is also a time of balance, with the days and nights being equal. Things come and things go. Life is cycles and flow. We feel energy rising within us just as it rises in the world, through the ground. It is the moment before everything bursts forth. Yet we instinctively feel the need to ground and center before jumping into the joyous dance of summer. We connect to the flow of spirit and feel how it moves through us and through the world. We seek to be steady channels for this energy, for the days of scarcity are not that far behind us and we still need to feel safe and secure.

> *Energy is matter that is transforming. Root yourself. Nothing is ever created, but everything just changes and flows in new forms. Breath deeply, then release: accept the flow of the Universe and became one with it.*

Keywords: possessiveness, guarding and managing resources, saving, protecting, stewardship
Reversed: greediness, hoarding, taking what isn't yours, misuse of or carelessness with resources

❧ FIVE OF PENTACLES ❧

Letting the unnecessary go

Suit meaning: coherence, stability, life, harmony
Number meaning: Beltane — a world growing a connection
Traditional meaning: poverty, need
Season: Spring giving way to Summer
Description: Two women, one young and one old, disrobe before entering a pond under a giant tree, their fingertips brushing. The roots of the tree are visible and reach into the water. Beneath the tree, all is dark and shady, but behind the tree is golden light. A bunny rests in the shadow of the tree.

Beltane is a celebration of connection, usually of opposites, which come together to create something new. It is a time of transformation. Before something can become something else, it must lose itself, let go of all that will not be needed in the future. It is a time of shedding, cleansing, and freeing. This is a voluntary poverty, a giving up of all that shaped our identity, of all that we used to create our sense of self. Thus naked, we find our true selves and are ready for connection, ready for spirit to work in and through us. Metamorphosis can be a anxious, frightening, or even painful experience. Fighting it makes it worse. Instead, the 5 of Pentacles invites us to welcome the experience to touch our true core and to see what we will become next.

> *To have more you need accept to have less. To receive you must first give. To wear new clothes, you must first get naked. There is nothing you really can't live without, as long as you live in harmony with the Universe. Spring gives way to summer, every year, no matter our age, or desires or our fears. After the rain, sun will just come.*

Keywords: poverty, lack, need, hunger, bankruptcy, ruin, destitution, health concerns, rejecting help, being blind to possible aid
Reversed: neglecting yourself or your finances, relying on charity unnecessarily, taking advantage of others

❧ SIX OF PENTACLES ❧

Be in the moment

Suit meaning: coherence, stability, life, harmony

Number meaning: Litha/Summer solstice — an explosion of beauty

Traditional meaning: generosity, equity

Season: Summer

Description: A beautiful blossoming tree is in the center of the card. A woman and a little girl are behind it. The girl is collecting fruits fallen to the ground. The woman is feeding a bunny. Gossamer threads connect everything.

At Litha the world explodes with beauty. The gloriousness of spirit and life is apparent everywhere. It is as if the generosity of the world is showing itself in its finest garb. Color, smells, and tastes satisfy our senses. Feeling thus satisfied, this sweet desire to give and to share flows through us as well. We are moved to share with the same abandon that nature does, while making sure we also enjoy a little for ourselves. The time of scarcity and darkness is long past and, at least for now, there appears to be enough for everyone.

> *Just be. Do not think. Do not move. Do not stop. Just be. And be yourself. Totally. And nothing else.*

Keywords: charity, fairness, gift, donation, grant, scholarship, loan, sound judgment, taxes, fees, sharing the wealth, asking for help

Reversed: denial of grant, loan, etc., stinginess, cheapness, uncharitable judgment, unfair taxes or fees, refusing to ask for or accept assistance, being unable to help when asked

∾ SEVEN OF PENTACLES ∾

Light at the end of the day

Suit meaning: coherence, stability, life, harmony

Number meaning: Lammas—the harvest in the world

Traditional meaning: the fruits of growth

Season: Summer giving way to Autumn

Description: A woman lets a squirrel climb on her shoulder, with a bunny under her feet. She is standing near a leafed tree in the middle of a grain field. On the tree is a pentacle and the connecting gossamer threads.

Lammas, the time of harvest, is a busy time. The days are beginning to shorten and we need to begin thinking of winter. Yet even in this time of activity, our connection to spirit reminds us to slow down and reflect, to learn from our recent experiences. Even the busy squirrel has taken time from his acorn gathering. It is important not to harvest too soon; everything needs time to mature. It is a good time to look at what we've done and determine whether the results were worth the effort. We can see what has worked well and what needs to be changed for the next time. There may even be time to adjust the results of the current harvest, if we take swift action.

> *Ends are precious moments, not sad moments. Ends give meaning to a journey. And even if they are not anything by themselves, they are necessary. Another word for "end" is "completion."*

Keywords: assessment, evaluation, reflection, measuring return on investment, harvest, rewards, appraisal

Reversed: disappointment, missed opportunity, harvesting too soon, plan didn't work out

≈ EIGHT OF PENTACLES ≈

Preparing the ligths

Suit meaning: coherence, stability, life, harmony
Number meaning: Mabon/autumn equinox—a world preparing to go to sleep
Traditional meaning: concentration on work
Season: Autumn
Description: A woman is carving a pentacle on a lamp. Many other lighted lamps are hanging from a beautiful tree. Red leaves cover the ground and float in the air.

The season of work is drawing to a close. This is the last of the long days, for tomorrow the darkness begins to overtake the light. We feel the last push to finish our projects, but even more than just finish or meet a deadline, we are driven to hone our skills, to do not just work but to do good work. We want to squeeze every minute from these remaining days and to make good use of them. This last burst of energy compels us, helps us find that our talents can be better than we think and that we have more to give than we imagined. We know that soon it will be time to rest, as the world falls asleep. We want to approach our beds with a clear conscience, knowing that we gave our all to the task at hand.

> *When night comes, it comes only to half of the world. You cannot live all your life in the light, but you can learn to see in darkness, and create lights for other to see as well. There is nothing to fear, and so much to be done.*

Keywords: work, skill, craftsmanship, artisan, diligence, dedication, focus, drive, determination, steady progress, satisfying work, attention to detail
Reversed: shoddy workmanship, workaholic, boring job, tediousness

≈ NINE OF PENTACLES ≈

The gentle silence

Suit meaning: coherence, stability, life, harmony

Number meaning: Samhain — a world asleep and open spiritual doors

Traditional meaning: inheritance and richness

Season: Autumn giving way to Winter

Description: A robed woman walks through water, her finger at her lips beckoning silence. There are grapes behind her and a colored bird is flying in the sky.

It has been a successful time and, indeed, abundant fruit is still all around us. There is still a little work to do and a little time to do it in. However, at Samhain there is a silence and reverence that we would do well to honor. It is easy to get caught up in the glorious abundance of nature and the wonderful results of our own labors. Instead, with the veil between the worlds so thin, we are asked to turn to our spiritual allies, the energy of the universe, and the God and Goddess, with gratitude. We are thankful for the gifts of the physical but we also listen with our hearts for the spiritual gifts that are offered to us at this time.

> *Let the world sleep sometimes. Move gently, without waking it up. See things as they are, peacefully waiting for the next day. There is a time for doing and a time for letting things go. Being there and being part of everything without the need to leave your mark on anything. There is magick in silence.*

Keywords: discipline, self-confidence, individual achievement, material wealth, safety, security, solitude

Reversed: not following through, dissatisfaction, looking for external praise

❧ TEN OF PENTACLES ❧

Continuity

Suit meaning: coherence, stability, life, harmony

Number meaning: the greater world

Traditional meaning: family through the generations

Description: Two dogs stand under a bower. An old man pets a cat and a young couple dances on a hill under a blue sky.

The seed of the Ace of Pentacles, with all its promises of abundance and stability and life, has blossomed in to fullness in the 10 of Pentacles. This is not the abundance of a season that will be consumed only to be replaced next year. This is prosperity, with roots deep in the earth creating a strong foundation for future growth. This is not fleeting emotions that ebb and flow but stable devotion and loyalty that stays true no matter the circumstances. This is an existence that has been carefully planted, nurtured, and protected over the years. Young and old, dog and cat, black and white, joy and contemplation, physical and spirit, they all exist in harmony creating a fullness that can face any trial, can provide whatever protection is needed, and can celebrate any joy with all the richness that the universe has to offer.

> *Among the strongest connections there is family. It does not bring only good or only bad, but it is a powerful force. The Universe linked us together with our parents, and will link us to our children, and then to their children. Around this channel of connections many more things have blossomed and will blossom.*

Keywords: family, connections, continuity, friendship, solidarity
Reversed: distance between family, division, not belonging

≈ SUIT OF WANDS ≈

Wands are linked to the powerful drive that comes from energy, passion and initiative.

Wands express the part of you that moves, that shakes, and that burns brightly. Creativity and expression are what fuels the greatest moments of any day.

Energy is ever flowing and dynamic. It never stops, but it may change pace, to allow for the quiet gathering of your forces or to explode in a powerful burst of passion.

In the Silver Witchcraft deck, the Wands are symbolized by Flames with a Silver core to them. They are like lanterns or benign fire spirits. They do not follow any regular pattern, but they bend to human will. For this reason, we are responsible of our actions and we are also responsible of our lack of actions. As long as the fires burn, it does not need to burn too strong. We choose our own rhythms to find the proper balance.

≈ ACE OF WANDS ≈

The spark that starts the fire

Suit meaning: energies, passions, drives, initiatives
Number meaning: the source of your passion
Traditional meaning: the source of fire/creativity
Season: none
Description: a burning flame fills the card with warmth and happiness. Around it many fruits of the harvest, symbols of abundance. An orange cat walks among the fruits.

Everything that is manifested in the physical world begins as a spark, an idea. The fruits of the harvest are the perfect symbol for this powerful seed. They have taken in the energy of the sun, our symbolic source of fire, and have turned it into matter, into something tangible, which, in turn, has a new seed inside. Fire can multiply; it is not a finite resource. When we connect with our own inner divinity, we have access to the Divine Fire of spirit. This fuels not only new ideas but provides passion and energy for life. It fires up our drive and strengthens our will. All of this is connected to our intuition, as represented by the cat. The Ace of Wands indicates a fresh idea, an exciting new project, or a burst of creativity or energy.

> *Energy is still energy even if not directed. Energy is a state of being. It is source, potential, vibrancy, edge. Energy is also contagious. There is nothing to be afraid with energy… it just makes everything brighter, faster, clearer, sharper. Including yourself.*

Keywords: desire, passion, will, drive, inspiration, potency, energy, enterprise, confidence, courage, optimism, setting goals, invention
Reversed: delay, dissatisfaction, lack of energy, impotence, a missed opportunity

≈ TWO OF WANDS ≈

The instant before the dawn

Suit meaning: energies, passions, drives, initiatives
Number meaning: Yule/Winter solstice — a world safe
Traditional meaning: contemplating options for expansion
Season: Winter
Description: A man stands in the mountains and overlooks the vastness before him. It's just before the dawn and the sun is breaking behind the mountains. He holds his hand so the sun appears to rest in his palm. An orange cat is sleeping around.

The longest night of the year is one of quiet contemplation and of faith. The next morning brings the new sun. Sometimes the contemplative life is very trying and we are eager to grasp the new day and begin creating. Sometimes we wait, impatient and poised, ready to begin work immediately. The 2 of Wands suggests that as soon as we see that tiny glimmer of light, feel the smallest encouragement, receive a little boost in energy, we should take it and move. The moment is not yet, but it is very near, so we shouldn't despise this time of considering and planning. Instead, we should use it wisely so that when the time right, we are ready to go.

> *Think of how movement starts. There an instant when you stop being still, and are not yet moving. It is the moment just before leaping. There is elation, and control… and suddenly the rush.*

Keywords: vision, energy, authority, ability, determination, dominance, intention, business or career proposal or decision, and confidence
Reversed: indecision, confusion, lack of vision, a business deal falls through

❧ THREE OF WANDS ❧

Birds flying north

Suit meaning: energies, passions, drives, initiatives
Number meaning: Imbolc—a world awakening
Traditional meaning: observing the unfolding of your initiatives
Season: Winter giving way to Spring
Description: in the morning, a man looks at the sea and watches a flock of migrating birds moving north. An orange cat greets the day with a long, slow stretch.

With the coming of Imbolc, the world is waking up and in the north, the lands are beginning to thaw. Birds start their long migration and other life begins to unfurl and stretch. The fire of life gathers the energy it needs to burst forth, from the hard shells of seeds, through the heavy earth, and the long, hard journey from womb to the outside world. Everything has stayed safe and warm, apparently static while inside great changes occur. The internal metamorphosis takes a lot of energy and even more is needed for that final push into new life. We can feel the tension, the energy quaking and quivering and gathering. Something wonderful is about to happen but it cannot be rushed.

A current starts slow, and then grows larger and faster and builds momentum. Things take time from the beginning to the moment they yield results. But the first, invisible step is perhaps the most important.

Keywords: optimism, expectation, attraction, Law of Attraction, prepared, culmination, return on investment, focus
Reversed: delay, discouragement, missed opportunity, poor judgment, bad decision, distraction, dissatisfaction

❧ FOUR OF WANDS ❧

Dancing around the fire

Suit meaning: energies, passions, drives, initiatives
Number meaning: Ostara/Spring equinox—a moment full of energy
Traditional meaning: celebration at the end of the day
Season: Spring
Description: A man and a woman with flowers in their hair are dancing around a fire. An orange cat is scuttling on the side, chasing his tail.

The winter is over and the days are getting longer. Winter has been well and truly survived and for this reason, we celebrate. The energy that has been building since Yule now feels like it has permission to burst forth and be articulated. Ostara, the Spring equinox, is a time of balance and before moving forward, the world shakes off the doldrums of winter in a spontaneous expression of energy and celebration. Soon enough, it will be time to focus that energy to the work at hand, but first, we shall dance just because we can.

> *It may be said that to really be in one place you need two things: "presence" and "focus." This card is about presence. Real presence. Not just merely being there. When people dance, you need to dance to really be there. When people eat, you must be eating. When people love, when people suffer, when people talk… you must be present. Not on the side, as an anonymous bystander.*

Keywords: holiday, party, celebration, gathering, honoring someone or something, successful completion of an endeavor, award ceremony, communal achievement
Reversed: plans go awry, celebrating too soon, discord, arguments

≈ FIVE OF WANDS ≈

The circle of life

Suit meaning: energies, passions, drives, initiatives
Number meaning: Beltane—a world of growing and connecting
Traditional meaning: struggles, competition and training
Season: Spring giving way to Summer
Description: On the sand, a few people of different ages and genders are holding hands together in a circle. Near them, two orange cats are scuffling with one another.

Sexuality is an apt metaphor for the energy of Beltane. The young, the strong, and the motivated come together to celebrate (and perhaps to create) life. Expanding the metaphor to life, it is a time to work together for the greater good, for the survival of the tribe. This means recognizing and utilizing each individual's talents and skills in the best possible way. Competition may be necessary to determine those strengths. An outcome may be that some need further training if they are to grow strong, just as seedlings need space and nourishment. Through mindful struggle, everyone can work to reach their highest potential and be prepared to face the coming growing season to the best of their abilities.

> *Remember that relationship with others is not without conflict. Win and lose. Smile and try again. There is no difference between the victor and the loser, unless we decide there is. There is no defeat, and no success. There is only growing.*

Keywords: competition, conflict, debate, group efforts, committees, strong personalities, differing opinions, no shared goal, lack of leadership
Reversed: fights, aggressiveness, willfully causing trouble, unproductive criticism

◦๑๑ SIX OF WANDS ๑๑◦

The nuptial procession

Suit meaning: energies, passions, drives, initiatives
Number meaning: Litha/Summer solstice — an explosion of beauty
Traditional meaning: heralding of accomplishments
Season: Summer
Description: a man and a woman are moving forward, their hands fastened together. Around them others hold torches. The man is carrying and orange kitten on his shoulder.

What a fortuitous event, a handfasting on the longest day of the year. Surely the young couple will be blessed with passion, ease, and abundance. During these halcyon days, everyone feels like kicking back and enjoying the early fruits of the earth and easy living. But getting to this place required hard preparation, seeds planted, sprouts tended. And a couple does not commit to each other without having done the hard work of getting to each other intimately enough to confidently make sacred vows that are witnessed by their community. The decision — for make no mistake, love is a decision if one is to love faithfully and not only when it's easy — to love someone in good times and bad is worthy of recognition and celebration.

> *When you start walking, you start a journey. And brief or long... straight or filled with turns (even u-turns), in known or unexplored paths... you still walk forward. Remember that even a first small step will one day bring you to an end of this road.*

Keywords: victory, honor, achievement, recognition, pride, public ceremony, accolades, accomplishment, success, triumph
Reversed: failure, being overlooked, disappointment, humiliation, dishonor, shame, taking credit for someone else's work

SEVEN OF WANDS

Preserving for the future

Suit meaning: energies, passions, drives, initiatives
Number meaning: Lammas—the harvest in the world
Traditional meaning: the last line of determination and defense
Season: Summer giving way to Autumn
Description: A family is storing part of the harvest for future use. A child plants a seed and a family of dogs is nearby.

So much bounty...and it can be a double-edged sword. For there is so much to enjoy. On the other hand, the more one has, the more one stands to lose. Also the days are growing noticeably shorter and the urgency of preparing for the winter falls upon us. In the 7 of Wands, this family begins storing their harvest, protecting themselves against the long days and nights of the winter's lack just as their loyal dogs are determined to protect them. This is a lovely picture of the cycle of life, with the mature harvest and the children and puppies, but is also a reminder that when we have something worth having, we need to work hard to keep it safe.

> *Defending will not bring security. We cannot control what the Universe will send to us, in good or in bad. So even when you prepare to close in, you must also look forward. Keep and hoard, but also give something back. Remember...even if the world was to end tomorrow it's still worth it to plant a tree today.*

Keywords: defending, protecting, valor, courage, standing up for beliefs, bravery, resolve, taking action
Reversed: defensiveness, overreacting, being easily offended, looking for a fight

⚜ EIGHT OF WANDS ⚜

Running against the wind

Suit meaning: energies, passions, drives, initiatives
Number meaning: Mabon/autumn equinox—a world preparing to go to sleep
Traditional meaning: motion
Season: Autumn
Description: a man is running widly, breathless and happy, against the strong wind without fatigue. Red leaves blow in the wind. An orange cat is startled awake and raises his head to look as the man runs near him.

The Autumn equinox brings a sense of urgency. There is so much left to do and so little time left to do it! The last of harvest must be brought in. So many loose ends to wrap up. That is the burden of great success; there is always something to attend to. And yet, it isn't a burden because everything is going just as it should. Plans we set in motion back in the Ace of Wands, months ago, are unfolding precisely as we wish and so we move through these last details and tasks with exhilaration. The end is almost here and it is going to be even better than we hoped. In the meantime, let's enjoy the rush!

> *The joy of the run. The breathless vertigo… elation sublime in just feeling your body. This is living the moment and not thinking about the future. Even if the wind blows against you, it's just the wind running opposite you and it will make you feel more alive.*

Keywords: speed, swiftness, events set in motion, travel, messages, communication, things running smoothly, reasonable consequences
Reversed: chaos, confusion, delays, frustration, swimming against the current

⚜ NINE OF WANDS ⚜

The hearth fire

Suit meaning: energies, passions, drives, initiatives
Number meaning: Samhain — a world asleep and open spiritual doors
Traditional meaning: warding, creating a border
Season: Autumn giving way to Winter
Description: People gather near a fire at twilight. An old man is telling a story, a cat sleeping in his lap, and the other are listening.

The twilight is an in-between time, a balance between dark and light, just like an equinox. Tomorrow the nights grow longer than the days and so we light a fire in an attempt to delay the dark as long as possible. The 9 of Wands suggests that establishing boundaries and protecting ourselves is appropriate now. The fire creates a boundary of light in the dark and helps us feel safe. We gather with those we trust and create a boundary of community. We listen to the wisdom of those with more experience so we can create our own inner light and develop discernment. Because the veil between worlds is thin, we carefully invite in the spirits we wish to communicate with but take precautions to keep out others.

> *We cannot learn any important thing fast. Take the time, to listen and to talk. Even to simply just be in silence. Slow down to a pace that is in harmony with that of the Universe. Savor the things you do, no matter how small they may be.*

Keywords: protecting, defending, stamina, loyalty, strength, discipline, wounded warrior
Reversed: hopeless cause, martyrdom, disloyalty, defensiveness, stubbornness

ꙮ TEN OF WANDS ꙮ

The fire burning under the snow

Suit meaning: energies, passions, drives, initiatives

Number meaning: the greater world

Traditional meaning: the burden and the journey

Description: Under the heavy snow, the fire has been reduced to burning embers. A man covered with snow, is walking toward the fire while carrying new timber, to get the fire burning again. With his other hand he is sheltering an orange cat on his chest, protecting him from the cold.

The spark that started the flame in the Ace of Wands has required careful tending and has waxed and waned with circumstances, including environmental changes and fuel resources. We grown to rely on it even though the early excitement has died out. Now, during a period of particular hardship, we find it difficult if not impossible to keep it burning. It has become an obligation and a burden rather than a joy. And yet, we love it still and cannot imagine our lives without it. So despite all the inconvenience, despite the incredible work involved, we will continue to tend it, this one particular flame, until we are ready to let it go out. When that happens, we will find another to light and to tend.

Potential and potential realized are connected. The fire is always burning just as you are still alive even if you are sleeping. You love even when you are not stating "I love you." But you need to give expression to things, you need to act, to create change and movement and to awaken. Remember that even in the coldest and darkest night, the Universe is beautiful.

Keywords: burden, obligations, numerous opportunities, duty, responsibility
Reversed: physical exhaustion, oppression, tyranny, subjugation

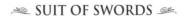

✧ SUIT OF SWORDS ✧

Swords are linked to the etheric world of communication, thoughts, words and rationalization.

It's a powerful suit, as Swords represent the more rational side of the human being, that very often rules our actions and relationship. We think, we learn, we calculate, we try to "be smart" and to face intelligently the challenges that life brings against us, or to use our smarts to take advantage of opportunities. Many times, however, the rational world we say we live in is just an excuse to cover emotions, needs and drives, sometimes very basic ones like shame, envy, self affirmation, lust, and greed. Swords also governs words and language, which are among our most powerful tools, which we can use to better humanity and create peace and harmony or we can we them to create illusions and hide behind them.

In the Silver Witchcraft, Swords are expressed by winged Athames. As any knife, an Athame can hurt, but it can also penetrate and clarify. And it's winged, because it can go much further than we think, when unburdened by our worst tendencies. It is a powerful symbol of hope. Of responsibility. Of awareness.

Without awareness, intelligence can be dangerous, but with awareness it becomes a blessing from the Universe.

⚖ ACE OF SWORDS ⚖

The source of words

Suit meaning: communication, rationality, intellect, responsibility, dealing with suffering and conflict
Number meaning: the source of your emotion
Traditional meaning: the source of reason
Season: none
Description: A winged Athame is suspended in the air, against a sun and moon sharing the sky. Colorful butterflies circle and spiral around the blade.

Ideas and reason are both powerful. Ideas create reality and reason is what we rely on (at least most of us in the Western world) to determine the truth about something. The athame (or sword), like ideas and reason, are double-edged. An idea can float through our minds, as light and elegant as a butterfly. That idea, if given a home in our minds, can change our world, for good or bad. Even the truth, usually considered a good or desirable thing, can be wielded with grace to create healing or with malicious intent and cause great pain. We can use our reason to determine the truth or we can use it to convince ourselves or others to believe a lie. We usually focus on solar reason, which is linear. This card reminds us that we have access to lunar reason, which is not linear but based on relationships between things and cycles. The Ace of Swords represents a wonderful and powerful gift, and we should be careful to use it responsibly.

> *There is no limit to what you can say with words. You can create ideas, express emotions, or just make something you see more real. Communication is not just between two people but can be between you and the Universe.*

Keywords: Logic, intellect, reason, truth, victory, decision, clarity, action plan, justice, knowledge, communication
Reversed: Indecision, faulty logic, kneejerk reaction, miscommunication, confusion, failure, injustice, a missed opportunity

ᔡ TWO OF SWORDS ᔡ

Trials and passages

Suit meaning: communication, rationality, intellect, responsibility, dealing with suffering and conflict
Number meaning: Yule/Winter solstice — a world safe
Traditional meaning: understanding the necessity of choice
Season: Winter
Description: in a snow field a blindfolded woman is sitting. She holds two different winged Athames in her hands. Footprints are in the snow behind her. Butterflies flit around the Athames, as if they were a source of nectar. Roses and lilies are blooming but freezing in the snow.

Yule is a season of celebration but there is something about the longest night of the year that encourages contemplation. We are so used to relying on our reason to make decisions, hundreds of them, every single day, that on the rare occasion that we actually slow down and reflect and listen to our hearts, we find that making the right decision isn't as clear and easy as we thought. Or perhaps we are facing choices that even after we've weighed out the pros and cons still feel equal. They both seem equal. The 2 of Swords recognizes that state and also acknowledges that a decision will need to be made. The advice given is to stop looking at the situation as usual. Our regular process is inadequate to the task. For this, we need to turn inward, to consult a different kind of reason.

> *When everything else is still, it is the moment just before movement takes place. Even in the harshest conditions, conflict could be transformed and used as an instrument to grow. The choices you make in difficult moments will brighten the road once the sun has returned.*

Keywords: needing to make a decision, insufficient data, lack of facts, denial, feeling conflicted, head and heart in opposition.
Reversed: ignoring facts, refusing to choose, lying to one's self

≈ THREE OF SWORDS ≈

Pain comes, pain goes

Suit meaning: communication, rationality, intellect, responsibility, dealing with suffering and conflict

Number meaning: Imbolc—a world awakening

Traditional meaning: understanding the existence of pain

Season: Winter giving way to Spring

Description: In the upper part of the card there are many roses and lilies that were frozen and are now melting. The water melting from them is making a waterfall and falling on the hands of a man below. Also on the ground there is a winged athame that is "piercing" a cup drawn into the snow.

Imbolc is considered a happy time because winter is beginning to melt away and we see a few signs of new life. Sometimes, though, it is our illusions that begin to melt. Something that we thought was true is revealed as false. We capture the icy water in our hands, shocked by the pain but still disbelieving, still clinging to our assumed reality. And then the truth pushes forth, like a seedling through the still cold soil, and we can no longer deny it. The dripping ice water has numbed us a bit, but still, the first plunge of this new truth into our hearts hurts. It pierces us in our core and nothing will ever be the same.

> *We cannot live a perfect life. Pain and suffering are part of the Universe. They will come and they will go. Pain is an experience. It may feel icy and cold, numbing your senses for a time, but it also awakens you to what is new and different.*

Keywords: unwelcome knowledge, painful truths, heartbreak, heartache, betrayal, disloyalty, unfaithfulness

Reversed: confusion, painful miscommunication, malicious words, hurtful lies, needless cruelty

❧ FOUR OF SWORDS ❧

Waiting for rebirth

Suit meaning: communication, rationality, intellect, responsability, dealing with suffering and conflict
Number meaning: Ostara/Spring equinox—a moment full of energy
Traditional meaning: understanding the need of silence
Season: Spring
Description: A woman crouches beside a tombstone with a pentagram on it. Above her is stained glass sun rising between two mountains. Around the tomb there is a little

snow, although spring has already come to the rest of this scene. A young woman, the sun shining on her face, places fresh flowers and an athame on the tombstone.

Ostara marks a time of gathered energy. We have been planning and preparing to burst into action since Yule. The sun has burst over the horizon and the drive to move propels us forward. However, before putting our noses to the grindstone and jumping feet first into action, something about this time of perfect balance reminds us to take a time for a moment of quiet, to contemplate the importance of both releasing and receiving. There are things that we've had to let go of over the harsh winter and we need to mourn them properly. We need to figure out how we will honor them in our hearts and minds and actions. In this way, we bring the memory forward with us but leave the parts that need to remain buried behind.

> *Things take time. Rebirth takes time. Healing takes time. Understanding takes time. Aging and growing takes time. Loving takes time. Something not yet completed is not imperfect... or wrong. Give time for things to come to you in their own natural time.*

Keywords: rest, retreat, meditation, peace, recovery, regrouping, careful consideration
Reversed: denial, useless obsessing, procrastination, disordered thinking

❧ FIVE OF SWORDS ❧

Impermanence

Suit meaning: communication, rationality, intellect, responsibility, dealing with suffering and conflict

Number meaning: Beltane –a world growing a connecting

Traditional meaning: understanding the need of victory and loss

Season: Spring giving way to Summer

Description: A man and woman, together, draw a line in the sand along with pentacles. The man's symbol is being erased by a wave. In middle of them is an athame stuck into the sand with a firefly on the hilt. The man and woman smile at each other.

During Beltane, the veil between the worlds is thin and we are able to more easily connect with the Otherworld to craft powerful magick that yields amazing results. It is also the moment when opposites come together to create something brand new. When faced with a situation that requires a winner and a loser, we can imagine the veil between us and our opponent is thin. We can try to see his point of view and feel his experience. We may even understand his goals. In doing so, we can perhaps craft a line that connects rather than separates. That line can lead to a situation in which not only both win but perhaps even a new solution is sparked that is equally exciting to both parties.

> *There are cycles in nature. Not just the seasons that flows regularly, but also tides and waves that move along the day and follow their own patterns. Something that we create is meant to last, and something else may only exist for a fleeting moment. But they still have the same importance.*

Keywords: victory, defeat, humiliation, aggression, good sportsmanship
Reversed: a pyrrhic victory, dishonor, poor sportsmanship

≈ SIX OF SWORDS ≈

Journey forward

Suit meaning: communication, rationality, intellect, responsibility, dealing with suffering and conflict
Number meaning: Litha/Summer solstice — an explosion of beauty
Traditional meaning: understanding the need to move forward
Season: Summer
Description: A boat sailing under a rainbow and past a waterfall. The man is moving the boat forward. The woman trails one hand in the water and waves in greeting with her other ahnd. The child watches the journey with anticipation. An athame and butterflies on the prow serve as a figurehead.

The longest day of the year provides enough illumination both to see what needs to be done and to have the time to do it. Not only that, but the first fruits of summer provide the resources we need to move from an undesirable situation to a better one. The weather is calm and the sun shines for hours, creating the perfect environment for taking the action that is needed. The journey might be long and maybe hard sometimes, but right now, it seems that everything is coming together so that our beginning is as easy as possible. The very beauty of the day is like a blessing on our undertaking.

> *We cannot always do the same things in the same way. Habits are a grave for the spirit. We must cross the river from past to future, from maybe to yes, from yesterday to tomorrow, from partial to all, from just one day to forever. Life is a journey and it goes only forward. For every thing lost, there are new things to gain and to learn. Because the Universe will always be bigger then our world.*

Keywords: journey, heading toward safety, escape, flight, travel, assistance, admitting defeat, impossible situation, protection, shelter
Reversed: remaining stuck, delay, worsening situation, unseen danger

✺ SEVEN OF SWORDS ✺

When the world pushes, you pull

Suit meaning: communication, rationality, intellect, responsibility, dealing with suffering and conflict
Number meaning: Lammas—the harvest in the world
Traditional meaning: understanding the need of indirect action
Season: Summer giving way to Autumn
Description: The wind is blowing many red leaves on the recently harvested field. A woman is clutching a tree to resist the strong wind, with her hair flowing. A puppy is trying unsuccessfully to overturn a turtle. An Athame is planted in the ground, a flower wrapping around it as a butterfly flits nearby.

Even during harvest, or perhaps especially during harvest, during our busiest times, things happen to upset the plan. And what great plans they were! We knew exactly what we wanted to do and when we needed to do it. Then, out of the blue, something blows in and our best laid plans are turned upside down. Sometimes we can work hard to put things back on track. Sometimes, though, there is nothing to be done but hold on tight and wait it out. After the storm has passed, we can assess the damage and regroup. Through slow and deliberate effort, we will eventually make our goal.

Force versus force. Unstoppable forces against immovable objects. So the "Titans" clash. But where is the wisdom of it? Think. Is it possible to walk against the wind? Yes. Is it possible to stop the wind from blowing? No.

Keywords: stealing, rescuing, stealth, dishonesty, sabotage, sneakiness, stealth, traitor, spy
Reversed: exposure, failure of dishonorable plan, caught in the act

❧ EIGHT OF SWORDS ❧

Ahead of the storm

Suit meaning: communication, rationality, intellect, responsibility, dealing with suffering and conflict

Number meaning: Mabon/autumn equinox — a world preparing to go to sleep

Traditional meaning: understanding the need of action

Season: Autumn

Description: Many ropes are tied to a bare tree. A storm is coming and geese are migrating south, trying to stay ahead of the storm. A woman is tied to the tree with a rope attached to her wrist. She is using her athame to free herself and escape the storm.

During the Spring equinox, we felt the need to slow down before summer burst upon us. The Autumnal equinox brings the opposite feeling. We need to take quick and decisive action before the world slows down and we are trapped. Over the season, we may have become attached to something that made us feel safe and grounded. But as the seasons change, as our life cycles ahead, our needs change. Because change is hard, we may stay tethered to something for too long, until, perhaps, it is almost too late. But we see and heed the signs and so we are not too late and we have what we need to free ourselves. A bit of quick thinking and common sense and we are out of the storm's path, safe and sound.

> *So many prisons are built by ourselves. We prefer to believe in what 100 people tell us rather than trust what the Universe is telling us. Even when the storm is approaching you may smile and just be free. Life is never a trap, it's always an experience.*

Keywords: feeling trapped, restricted, dangerous situation, limited options, helplessness, complex problems

Reversed: victim mentality, giving up, seeing problems where none exist

❧ NINE OF SWORDS ❧

The sound of silence

Suit meaning: communication, rationality, intellect, responsibility, dealing with suffering and conflict

Number meaning: Samhain — a world asleep and open spiritual doors

Traditional meaning: understanding the existence of consequences

Season: Autumn giving way to Winter

Description: A woman stands near a bed and is opening a window to the outside. Outside it's snowing and the snow is coming inside. The blanket on the bed is embroidered with a tree and an athame lies on the bed.

It is night and time to rest the body and renew the mind. However, we find that difficult on this particular night. The veil between the worlds is very thin right now. Messages from beyond flow more easily into our minds. Our hearts yearn with a desire to connect with those on the other side. So we waken and reach out, seeking and sometimes finding that sweet connection, hearing voices from the past, receiving answers and guidance from those whose love is no less real even though it is not of this world. Not all voices are meant for us and not all guidance is good. We need to exercise discernment to know what to cling to, what will feed our spirits and to know what to let fall to the ground unbidden.

> *When you open a window, there is more space and more air, but also the cold may come inside. Still, it is impossible to contain our world in one enclosed space and be complete. Even if it's cold, we need to connect and reach outward. Sometimes it's a communication without sound, just like an evening when it's snowing and all appears still and peaceful.*

Keywords: obsessive thoughts, sleeplessness, nightmares, worries, guilt, despair, oppression

Reversed: insomnia, over-use of sleeping aids

❧ TEN OF SWORDS ❧

In the end, the beginning

Suit meaning: communication, rationality, intellect, responsibility, dealing with suffering and conflict
Number meaning: the greater world
Traditional meaning: understanding the need of endings
Description: In a clearing in the middle of the woods, there are 10 athames planted into the ground. Many butterflies fly around. The darkness of the foreground gives way to sunlight and color in the distance.

Endings are a natural part of life, even though they aren't always easy or pleasant. As we first approach the reality of an ending in our life, it is like running up against a spiked wall, separating what was from what is to be. The wall is dark and foreboding and so we assume what is on the other side is as well. As we become used to the wall, we realize it is not a wall at all, but just a moment of transition as what was changes, as everything in life changes. Theses changes happen every day but we don't see them because they are so small. Then one day, they seem to coalesce into this huge wall. But we step through the wall which isn't a real wall. And we step again. The light changes. A new world emerges, different, perhaps, but still full of beauty and mysteries waiting to be explored.

> *The mind is a powerful tool for transformation. Even if reality changes and things are now different, they won't be really until our mind accepts it. And if our mind is ready for change, for ends and new beginnings, then it's the time when end and new beginnings will happen.*

Keywords: surrender, ending, disaster, defeat, ruin, stop fighting, giving in, giving up, acknowledging an ending
Reversed: melodrama, refusing to let go, denial

CHAPTER 6:
THE COURT CARDS

The Court cards each feature a person and quite simply represent the people in our lives. They can also represent aspects of yourself. Learning to tell the difference comes easily after a little experience. You will find that you will intuitively know when a Court card is another person or part of your own personality. Just as people are complex, so are the Court cards. However, they represent only one facet of a personality and real humans are multi-faceted, so they are easier to understand that actual people.

Keep in mind that while each Court has either a male or female on it, in tarot gender is symbolic not literal, so the King of Silver Wings could represent a woman and the Queen of Silver Moons could represent a man. Age is also symbolic, so a Page can be an older person but one who is less experienced or who lacks confidence in a certain area.

Reflection

Every person holds within himself or herself a little bit of each of the Courts. We just express our way of being in different ways depending on the situation and on the social context, but what we express is always a part of us. An old and dignified doctor (maybe a King of Wands in our expectations) may behave in a childish and easygoing way with his nephews (like a Page of Chalices) or be aggressive and loud when watching the Superbowl on TV (like a Knight of Swords).

If you want to understand the Court Cards better, think of them as part of yourself, as attitudes, as expressions of different approaches to life and to various situations.

Just like people, the Court cards have their positive qualities and their negative aspects. If you are using reversals, the negative aspects generally apply. If you do not use reversals, then you will rely on the surrounding cards and your intuition to decide if the positive or negative qualities will come into play for the reading. Because these cards represent people, there are no keywords associated with them.

The basic qualities of the Court cards are determined by four elements: their suit, their rank, Feeling/Doing, and Learning/Knowing. You are already familiar with the suits, so the following ideas will feel familiar.

- People of the **Silver Moons** are creative, empathetic, sympathetic, nurturing, sensitive, loving, intuitive, and caring. They are emotional and value relationships. They can also be needy, demanding a lot of attention from others in their lives, as well as overly sensitive and easily hurt.

- People of the **Silver Threads** are practical, loyal, and stable. They tend to value money, resources, and creature comforts. Luckily, they are also often good managers of such things. Because of their connection with the physical world, they can seem shallow. In addition, their precise accounting can lead to pettiness and their stability can turn into dullness or stagnation.

- People of the **Silver Wings** are problem-solvers and plan-makers. They are often precise, witty, clever, intelligent, and excellent communicators. Sometimes they appear as cold-hearted and distant. Because they are so discerning, they are quick to pick up on weaknesses and can be known for their sharp tongues and cutting words.

- People of the **Silver Flames** are known for their charisma, energy, optimism, charm, leadership, and warmth. They can be driven and passionate. They can also be self-centered, always wanting to be the center of attention. Their warm personality may turn to anger in a flash, making them rash, immature, or cruel.

Ranks are also easy to learn, as they follow a hierarchy of authority and power that you would expect with names such as Knight and Queen.

- **Pages** are young, either chronologically or in terms of experience or confidence. They are curious and enthusiastic but may require a lot of attention or handholding.

- **Knights** are a bit more experienced and very driven. They may bite off more than they can chew and be so focused that they don't see the big picture.

- **Queens** are mature, confident, and caring. They are most comfortable with one on one relationships and can become self-absorbed.

- **Kings** are also mature and extremely confident, sometimes to a fault. They see the big picture and are interested in group dynamics rather than individual relationships.

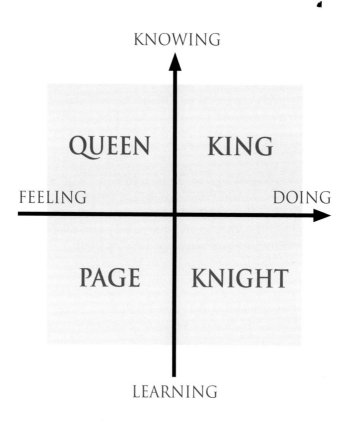

Pages: Feeling/Learning
Knights: Learning/Doing
Queens: Knowing/Feeling
Kings: Knowing/Doing

Feeling/Doing and Learning /Knowing

These pairs are different, more nuanced ways of describing the cards as either "active" or "passive," which is a traditional way of describing them.

- Feeling is passive and doing is active. Feeling is an internal experience. Doing is an external experience.

- Learning is active and knowing is passive. Learning relies on exploring the external world while knowing assumes an internal completeness.

So the Knights, being both "learners" and "doers," are the most active of the bunch. The Queens, being "knowers" and "feelers," are the most passive.

Reflection

In the Court Cards there are several recurring elements that depend both on the suit and on the rank.

The Element of the Suit is represented by an Elemental Spirit: an Undine for Chalices, a Gnome for Pentacles, a Salamander for Wands and a Sylph for Air. They are the same elementals standing in front of the High Priest in the Arcana number V. The Element is also represented by the background... be it water, sand, grass or clouds.

The four Pages all have a playful appearance. They have the ability to enjoy the present moment to the fullest.

The four Knights are always mounted on a steed, and the Elemental is close to their arms to express the dynamic "let's do it" nature of the cards.

The four Queens keep the symbol of the suit close to their lap, near their womb. In the Queen cards, the elemental is often free to do as it pleases, under the watchful and benevolent attention of the Queen.

The four Kings are on a throne as the Queens (but their throne is more artificial and sophisticated than the natural looking ones of the Queens) and the elemental near them is always creating or releasing something or letting something.

ᔋ PAGE OF CHALICES ᔋ

The Dreamer

Learning and Feeling about Emotions
Description: A female in a blue ritual robe under a triple moon and standing knee deep in water. She is holding a chalice high and smiling brightly while an undine plays in the water around her.

The Page of Chalices is a sensitive individual, curious about relationships and opening up to her feelings. In fact, she learns about the world and herself by focusing on her feelings. She is interested in exploring the mysteries of life and is very open to psychic and metaphysical ideas. She is creative and imaginative and expresses her creativity and imagination freely. She can be overly sensitive, retiring, and shy and can sometimes willfully ignore common sense or rational arguments.

Reflection
Dreaming is about a connection between our desires and reality. Some dreams may be a seed of something more, and others will just disappear to be woven anew into different dreams inside our heart.

❧ KNIGHT OF CHALICES ❧

The Artist

Learning and Doing about Emotions
Description: A male in a blue ritual robe is riding a dolphin through the sea under a triple moon. She is holding a chalice high, while an undine is wrapping around her other arm.

The Knight of Chalices is a dreamer and a romantic. He feels things deeply and commits readily. Once committed to a quest, he rarely gives up, holding true until the end. He is moved by art and may be an artist himself. He holds the feelings of heart above all else and will not be dissuaded by logical arguments or common sense. He can be so focused on what he feels to be true and his own emotions that he ignores reality.

> Reflection
> *Art is a dream made real. Not a plan, or a project, but something truly made from the stuff of dreams, speaking the language of dreams, touching our emotions without concern for rationality and sense. This is also the reason why sometimes art is not understood, or dismissed as something of no consequence.*

✦ QUEEN OF CHALICES ✦

The Confidant

Knowing and Feeling about Emotions
Description: A female in a blue ritual robe
with a crown is sitting on a throne of sea-
shells that rises out of the sea, with a chalice in her hands. The triple moon shines
overhead and an undine is playing a harp
beside her throne.

The Queen of Chalices is a quiet, intro-
verted woman who loves art and beautiful
things. She may be a patron of the arts. She
is usually very psychic and intuitive, usual-
ly sensing the feelings of others around her. It is easy to become intimate with
her, as she can understand different points of view. Her sensitivity, a great gift,
can be a burden as she can easily become over-stimulated or influenced by the
energy around her. To protect herself she turn toward self-involved, obsessing
over her own emotions while ignoring those of others.

> Reflection
> *Confidence is a sharing of secrets, of small and big things that are close to
> our heart and as such are fragile and important. They say that to receive
> a confidence is to take the responsibility of treading gently over someone
> else emotions. Sometimes people of exceptional sensibility can perceive se-
> crets and emotions, just like they received a confidence.*

✎ KING OF CHALICES ✎

The Healer

Knowing and Doing about Emotions
Description: A male in a blue ritual robe and a crown is sitting on a throne of rocks that rises out of the sea. He is under the triple moon and holds a chalice. An undine next to him is pouring fishes from a bowl into the sea.

The King of Chalices has a love of family and is committed to any groups or organizations he belongs to. He is quiet and may come across as unemotional or distant, but he has deep feelings. He makes decisions based on his emotions but sometimes on his intuition as well, although he is not as comfortable with this as the Queen. In fact, he sometimes fights against his natural gifts because he, for whatever reason, has but taught or decided they are not valid. Still, nothing dampens his love of the arts and he often supports creative ventures.

Reflection
Time heals, but it doesn't heal alone. Emotion can have scars as much as the body but even more insidious as they are more difficult to see. The power to heal and help someone else is a powerful gift. It requires patience and wisdom, and empathy with all kind of sorrows.

ᴥ PAGE OF PENTACLES ᴥ

The Apprentice

Learning and Feeling about Stability
Description: A female in green robes is standing on a big gold coin on the ground. There is grass and flowers everywhere, and a gnome is standing still in the middle of flowers. The woman is eating grapes.

The Page of Pentacles is innocently sensual. That is, she loves the beauty of the world and enjoys the fruits of the earth. She is sweet and open to seeing the best in everything and everyone. Consequently, others are attracted to her charming enthusiasm and want to share things with her. Her challenge is not getting too caught up in material things and losing sight of the spiritual. Greediness and laziness are rare in her, but they can surface from time to time.

Reflection
Focusing on practice rather than theory and learning by example rather than by words. This may be applied to many things, not just work and crafts, but even in the way you relate to others. Sometimes it is just necessary to "be there", before anything else can happen.

✺ KNIGHT OF PENTACLES ✺

The Orderer

Learning and Doing about Stability
Description: A male in green robes is riding a stag and sounding a horn. The stag is standing on a big gold coin in the ground in the middle of forest and there are threads connecting the coin to the stag and rider. A gnome is riding in front of the man. Flowers blossom on the footsteps of the stag.

Like the other Knights, the Knight of Pentacles is focused. However, out of all the Knights, he is the slowest, the most cautious. To some, he may seem dull and slow, but he is always very aware of what is going on around him. He watches and assesses, and when the time is right, he takes action. His diligence is usually rewarded, as beautiful and useful things follow in his wake. If not motivated, he can become materialistic, boring, and plodding.

> Reflection
> *Everything should find its proper place. Order is not something that can't ever change, but every moment all things should be in their proper place, to allow for a smooth connection between all things and their use.*

꧁ QUEEN OF PENTACLES ꧂

The Preserver

Knowing and Feeling about Stability
Description: A female with green robes and
a crown is sitting on a throne made within
a tree. She has a big coin in her lap and
there are threads everywhere. A gnome is
carving the side of the throne and a bunny
is bringing flowers to the naked feet of the
queen.

The Queen of Pentacles is calm, serene,
and grounded. She has a clear understanding of the world and how it works and how
she works within it. She is practical but still insists on beauty and values skill,
talent, and fine workmanship. She nurtures everyone and everything around
her, bringing out their very best. She attracts abundance. Like the other Pentacles court, she can become materialistic if she loses sight of her ideals. Despite
her apparent serenity, she is ambitious and can be overly so from time to time.

Reflection
Even if it impossible to keep what we love from harm, we would still try.
Sacrifice, attention, benevolence... they cannot alone make happiness in
others, but they are a fertile ground where happiness is easier to blossom.

✒ KING OF PENTACLES ✒

The Provider

Knowing and Doing about Stability
Description: A male with green robes and a
crown is sitting on a throne made of perfectly carved wood. He has a big coin that
he holds with both hands. A gnome is taking seeds from a pouch and sending them
around.

The King of Pentacles is very comfortable in the world. Not only has he created prosperity and comfort in his own life,
but he helps others create it in theirs. He is
generous and kind-hearted, a wonderful and gracious host. He values family
and the past but always looks ahead, planning for the future. He can tend toward materialism and ambition or overindulge in the gifts of the world.

> Reflection
> *Sometimes it is important to go past the individual needs of any person,*
> *and look at the needs of a greater group. Understanding how to allocate*
> *resources and differentiate between what is necessary now and what will be*
> *useful later. Accepting this role is a burdensome task, and requires paying*
> *attention to the needs of others.*

✑ PAGE OF WANDS ✑

The Inventor

Learning and Feeling about Creativity
Description: A female in a red robe stands in the desert with the silver fire in her hands and smiling brightly. A salamander is playing in the sand next to her.

The Page of Wands is a very enthusiastic and energetic person. She loves to be involved in the action. She is brave, sometimes to a fault, taking risks but usually coming out on top due to her determination and charisma. She is a whirlwind of energy, hard to keep up with and hard to control. She is warm and passionate, but her feelings can turn quickly if things don't go her way.

> Reflection
> *Everything that is new needs to be invented, tried, savored, risked. Playing with fire may be a bit risky, but such wild enthusiasm it is the only way to open the doors of creativity.*

KNIGHT OF WANDS

The Traveller

Learning and Doing about Creativity
Description: A male is riding a camel in the desert, with a silver fire in his hand and a salamander on his arm. He is pointing forward and following tracks in the sand. There are pyramids in the distant background.

The Knight of Wands is extremely passionate and once he has determined to do something, he will do it with focused determination. Although he prefers to moves quickly, and often does, he also has the stamina to see his projects through, unless he becomes distracted by something else. He is very curious and interested in so many things that it is easy for him to lose that incredible focus.

> Reflection
> *As the world is bigger than our experience, the Traveler explores the world, everyday one step further, changing and enlarging his confines as he defies his own limits.*

≈ QUEEN OF WANDS ≈

The Muse

Knowing and Feeling about Creativity
Description: A female is on a throne rock made of sand holding a silver fire in her lap. She has a crown. A salamander near her is using some gems to make a nest and basks in the sun.

The Queen of Wands is an intense and passionate woman. She understands her own power and isn't afraid to use it to get what she wants. She is fiercely loyal and will use her gifts to help those she loves. Like the Queen of Chalices, she is very intuitive but is more practical and less dreamy. And unlike the Queen of Chalices, she has no problem protecting herself from unwanted external influences. She is a great friend but a dangerous enemy.

> Reflection
> *Inspiration is another key to creation. But even if we are not able to create something, each and every idea that comes from us or to us will be transformed and changed into a different seed that will take hold somewhere.*

≈ KING OF WANDS ≈

The Architect

Knowing and Doing about Creativity
Description: A male is on a throne made of gems holding a silver fire with both hands. A salamander has untied a knot that held closed a sack full of riches. A single palm tree is keeping the king in shadow, protecting him from the heat.

The King of Wands is very driven. He is a man of great vision, able to see incredible possibilities in the worst of circumstances. Through the sheer power of his will, he is able to turn sand into treasure and release great abundance into whatever he sets his hand to. He recognizes and values talent in others but has no patience for those who won't work. His passion can turn to impatience and to anger if he feels he's been let down.

Reflection
The greatest things have not been created in a day. A true Architect understands the need of planning and patience and let things grow slowly and steadily until they are completed.

❧ PAGE OF SWORDS ❧

The Student

Learning and Feeling about Rationality
Description: a female with yellow robes is standing in the middle of the clouds with a winged athame in her upraised hand. She is smiling brightly and a sylph is offering her a closed book.

The Page of Swords is smart, witty, and quick. She loves learning, which comes very easily to her. Her mind is concise, precise, and logical. She has a strong sense of justice and values the truth. Sometimes she lives too much in her mind, forgetting to take into account the feelings of others. She likes to argue and debate for the fun of it but can take it too far, hurting other's feelings.

> Reflection
> *There are many ways of learning, just as there are many ways to be intelligent. The Student focuses on learning with the mind and she finds joy from the sheer knowledge that she has found.*

KNIGHT OF SWORDS

The Achiever

Learning and Doing about Rationality
Description: a male with yellow robes is riding an eagle in the middle of clouds with a winged athame brandished as if it were a sword. He has a book in his other hand. There are stars in the sky and he is riding toward the Polar Star.

Like all Knights, the Knight of Swords is focused and once he knows where he wants to go, nothing can stop him. He is the fastest moving of all the Knights. His wit and tongue are as fast as he is and he loves to show off his cleverness. He isn't boasting, though, because he really is highly intelligent. However, he doesn't always realize that not everyone is as committed to logic as he is. He can see the world in black and white, missing all the shades in between.

Reflection
Aim higher, go faster, do better. The Achiever within us always drives ourselves further, not because of curiosity but because of ambition. He measures himself only against challenges and believes in his own strength.

QUEEN OF SWORDS

The Critic

Knowing and Feeling about Rationality
Description: A female with yellow robes is sitting on a throne made of rock that is surrounded by clouds. She has a crown. And holds an athame in her lap.
Nearby, a sylph is writing in an open book with a big paintbrush.

The Queen of Swords is clear-headed and smart. She has learned through life experience as well as through study and marries both to great effect. She shares her wisdom with others, counseling and guiding her friends and loved ones through hard times. She is a great planner and problem-solver. Because she has come through so much herself, she loses patience with those who are not willing to address their own challenges. She can have a sharp tongue, for she always tells the truth. If you don't want to know, then don't ask.

Reflection
The ability not to accept everything at face value, but to think for yourself and make up your own mind belongs to the Critic. She accepts not just her limits, but also the limits of others, and always traces her own road to each and every opinion.

❧ KING OF SWORDS ☙

The Judge

Knowing and Doing about Rationality
Description: A male with yellow robes and a crown, holding an athame with both hands, is sitting on a throne made of beautifully sculpted stone that emerges from the clouds. Next to him a sylph is reading from an open book placed on a pedestal.

The King of Swords loves efficiency and justice. His keen mind and strong sense of right and wrong guide all his decisions and actions. He is careful to be sure of his own mind before he speaks, so although he is an excellent communicator, he is often silent, assessing all sides and not merely reacting. He is an excellent organizer and often believes his way is the right way. Even though his is often the right way, he can be bossy and manipulative, convincing others to do what he wants.

Reflection
In the real world, it is sometimes necessary to make a decision about what is right and what is wrong. It is a difficult, dangerous and lonely road, which can only be sustained by perfect fairness.

CHAPTER 7:
SPREADS

Spreads are also called layouts. They are what gives a reading structure. A spread illustrates how the cards are laid out on the table and what the position of each card means. The question asked, the card, and its position shape the final meaning you give the card in a reading. Your intuition also plays a role and should be folded into all the information to help determine the interpretation. The position in which the cards are laid out is important as well because this shows how the energy of each card interacts with the energy of the surrounding cards. Cards next to each other have a certain relationship, like partners, while cards in a vertical line represent more of a hierarchical relationship. As you interpret the cards, notice if the figures are facing each other, in the same direction, or away from each other. This can help you determine if the energy is in conflict, blending, or moving in the same direction.

Spreads range from simple to complex, as you will see. Some given here reflect the needs of the situation and require multiple steps. Others make use of the specific divisions of the deck and require that you separate them into smaller decks. Spreads are useful and most published spreads have the benefit of having been used and proven useful by other readers. However, you should feel free to experiment and create your own or modify ones that you find in books or online.

The spreads here will begin with the most simple and increase in complexity. You will see that both types can give very good advice and information. Indeed, some readers find they get clearer answers with fewer cards, because too many cards creates confusion, while other readers find that more cards provide more information that they can form into fuller answers. Experiment and find out which kind suits your reading style.

≈◦ ONE CARD SPREAD ◦≈

One card spreads are the easiest, but that doesn't make them less useful. As you know, each card is a key to vast wisdom, so one card can be enough to sufficiently answer a question.

The one card spread isn't really a spread but more of a technique. You simply ask your question and draw one card.

One card spreads during a day
A card in the morning: what should I pay attention to, today?
A card in the evening: what should I learn from what happened to me today?

THREE CARD SPREADS

Three cards spreads are favorites among tarot readers as they are the happy medium between too few and too many cards. In addition, the positional meanings can easily be changed to suit a variety of needs.

Most three card spreads are laid out:

The most common three card spread is:

🍃 1. **Past:** energy from the past that is influencing the current situation

🍃 2. **Present:** current energy that is at the center of the situation

🍃 3. **Future:** the most likely outcome if everything remains as it is

It is important to note that all spreads with an "outcome" position show only probable outcomes, as the future is not set in stone. If the outcome is not to your liking, it may be possible to change it by taking action. By using the reading technique explained earlier, you can see to what extent it is possible to change. Do further readings to see how actions might alter the outcome.

Other positional meanings for the Three Card Spread include:

If you are facing a decision between two choices, this can be a helpful spread. If you have more than two choices, add more cards to represent them all.

- ❧ **1. Choice A:** information needed about Choice A
- ❧ **2. Your attitude:** about the situation
- ❧ **3. Choice B:** information needed about Choice B

When deciding what to do about a situation, get advice from these positions.

- ❧ **1.** What to do
- ❧ **2.** What not to do
- ❧ **3.** What you need to know

For a snapshot of how you are doing in general, many reader like this one.

- ❧ **1.** Body
- ❧ **2.** Mind
- ❧ **3.** Spirit

As you can see, this is a very flexible and adaptable way to lay out the cards and can be changed to meet a number of needs.

This is a traditional spread with many variations. As you work with it, feel free to change any of the positional meanings, particularly the ones on the right, to suit your needs.

- **1. You:** how you feel about the situation
- **2: Past:** energy from the past affecting the situation
- **3: Additional information:** extra information that can help clarify the situation
- **4. Present:** energy in the present that is at the center of the situation
- **5. Challenge:** something that may be blocking the situation
- **6. Future:** energy in the future that should be taken into account as you move forward
- **7. Outcome:** the probable outcome

NEW MOON SPREAD

This is a great spread to do at the New Moon, to see what energies we should focus on during the upcoming lunar cycle.

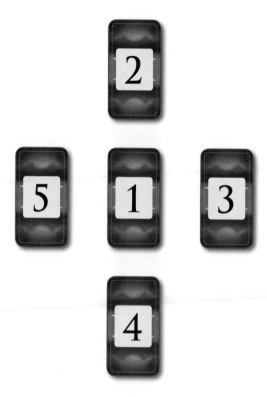

- 🌙 **1. Theme:** the theme that will be present in your life during this cycle
- 🌙 **2. New Moon:** the seed that is planted
- 🌙 **3. Waxing Moon:** what is growing
- 🌙 **4. Full Moon:** what manifests
- 🌙 **5. Waning Moon:** what to release

This spread is also useful if we are thinking about manifesting something specific rather than seeking general information. Use these positional meanings to learn more about a project you have planned.

1. **Project:** for this position, go through your deck and select the card that best represents what you want to manifest.
- 2. **New Moon:** how to set your intention
- 3. **Waxing Moon:** how to nurture your project
- 4. **Full Moon:** what you need to do to complete your project
- 5. **Waning Moon:** what you need to eliminate or edit from your project

⚜ SABBAT SPREAD ⚜

As magickal practitioners, one of the reasons we celebrate the sabbats is to "help turn the wheel," as it were. Not that nature needs our help but it is one way we stay in alignment with nature. This spread can be used for any of the Sabbats.

❧ 1. **Theme:** for this position, take the four cards (one from each of the suits) that represents the Sabbat you are preparing for. For example, the 2s for Yule, the 3s for Imbolc, and so on. Shuffle them and draw one. This is the particular facet of the sabbat for you to focus on this year.

Shuffle the other three cards back into the deck and draw the rest of the cards as usual.

❧ 2. **Foundation:** understanding that you already have and should build on this year

❧ 3. **Aspiration:** this is what you should reach for this year

❧ 4. **Release:** this is what you should release this year

❧ 5. **Action:** this is the action you should take to help turn the wheel this year

This spread is inspired the common Astrological Houses Spread, where cards are drawn and laid in a circle like an astrological chart and the positions are the same as the Houses. Here, we use the Wheel of the Year. This spread has two variations, much like the New Moon Spread, one that can be used for a general overview and one that can be used for a specific project.

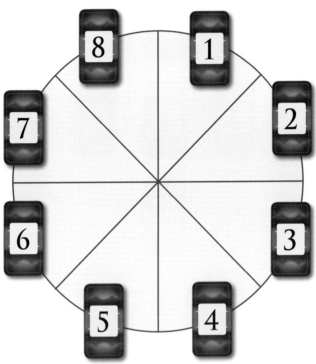

- 1. Yule
- 2. Imbolc
- 3. Ostara
- 4. Beltane
- 5. Litha
- 6. Lammas
- 7. Mabon
- 8. Samhain

General Variation

The card in each position indicates what you can expect to culminate at that sabbat date. Read the energy of the previous sabbat as waning as you move toward the next.

Specific Project Variation

The only difference in the layout is that you first go through your deck and select a card that represents your project and put it in the middle of the circle. Then you use the positional meanings as described below.

- 1. **Yule:** what to welcome to the project
- 2. **Imbolc:** how to nurture the project
- 3. **Ostara:** how to increase the project
- 4. **Beltane:** what to enjoy about the project
- 5. **Litha:** the first fruits, which will encourage you as continue on
- 6. **Lammas:** the second harvest, which will satisfy you and create abundance
- 7. **Mabon:** the final harvest, which will sustain you and provide seeds for the future
- 8. **Samhain:** what to release

Many magickal practitioners do a divination before doing any magickal work to see if the spell will have the results they intend. This spread is done in steps. The number of steps depends on the outcome at each stage.

Step One
First, work out the spell you plan on working. If you are working magick, you should be familiar with all the possible ramifications and ethics involved. Think them through ahead of time, as usual, and then use these spreads to verify. If things don't look like they'll go as planned, rework your spell or change your intent until you get a satisfactory reading. Once you are clear on your intent and your spell, do the following reading to determine the results of your work, should you perform it:

Read the three cards together to determine the outcome. If you find it satisfactory, move on to the final step, Spell Preparation Spread. If not, do Step Two to discern the problem.

Step Two

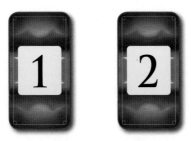

- 1. **Intent:** this card will show if there is a problem with your intention
- 2. **The Spell:** this card will show if there is a problem with your spell itself

It is possible that there is a problem with both or with neither. If there is no discernable problem, no area that can be altered or modified, then reconsider doing this magick at all. It may not be in your best interest or for the greatest good to continue with it. If there is a problem with one or the other or both, rethink your intent and/or you spell and repeat Steps One and Two until you are satisfied. Once you are, then move onto the Spell Preparation Spread.

≈ SPELL PREPARATION SPREAD ≈

For this spread, you will divide your deck into five piles, the Major Arcana and the suits of the Minor Arcana. Cards 1, 2, and 3 are drawn from the Majors. Card A will be drawn from the Silver Wings (Swords). Card B from the Silver Flames (Wands). Card C from the Silver Moons (Cups). Card D from the Silver Threads (Pentacles). If your tradition uses different elemental associations for the directions, simply modify this to reflect your own practices.

The spread is designed to look like an altar. Each of these positions represents the best aspect to invoke for the work you propose to do.

- 1. The Divine
- 2. The Goddess
- 3. The God
- A. The Guardian of the East, Air
- B. The Guardian of the South, Fire
- C. The Guardian of the West, Water
- D. The Guardian of the North, Earth

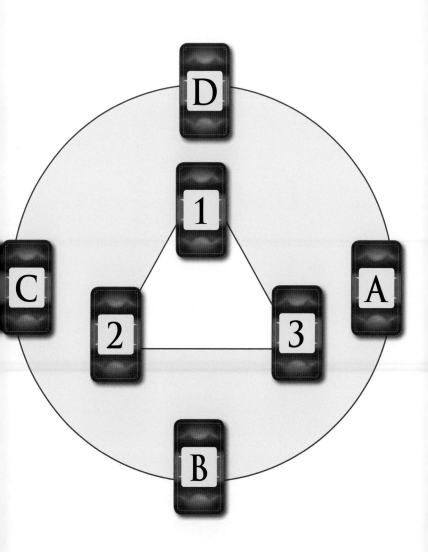